Praise for *Public Hig...*

"Wallerstein, a successful college president from whom others can learn a great deal, gives us hope that Baruch's successful strategies can be replicated on other campuses. This volume is a valuable case study on the role of leadership in addressing critical higher education issues—from financial and physical space challenges to the academic performance of first generation/immigrant college students. I highly recommend it."
—**Freeman A. Hrabowski III**, president emeritus, University of Maryland, Baltimore County

"In this compelling case study of Baruch College of The City University of New York, president emeritus Mitchel Wallerstein provides invaluable perspective on the potential of public higher education. Owing in no small measure to his decade at the helm, Baruch has succeeded in developing an institutional culture characterized by academic excellence and economic stability—as he puts it, a "positive outlier" among peer institutions. His assessment of whether other public colleges and universities can replicate the enviable successes of Baruch should serve to inspire academic leaders of all institutional types as well as all those committed to the advancement of public higher education."
—**Michael M. Crow**, president, Arizona State University

"Mitchel Wallerstein has done an exceptional job capturing the remarkable success of Baruch College, a gem of The City University of New York. While it's no surprise that Baruch is often cited as a leading engine of social and economic mobility because of both its high quality and affordability, it is, as Dr. Wallerstein notes, a surprise that its story is not more widely known. I hope this book and its lessons help remedy that oversight."
—**James B. Milliken**, chancellor, The University of Texas System

"Today more than ever before, the United States needs high quality, affordable public higher education. Unfortunately, we live in a time when all public colleges face serious, unrelenting academic, financial, and political challenges. Yet despite the difficult environment, a few public institutions have gotten stronger academically, increased their financial stability, and become more desirable to students and families who are choosing a college. Mitchel Wallerstein's crisp and thorough account of how Baruch College of The City University of New York (CUNY) has flourished while others have stumbled makes for gripping reading and provides a road map that other schools should consider."
—**Terry W. Hartle**, senior fellow, American Council on Education

"*Public Higher Education That Works* offers a deeply contextual and compelling success story demonstrating the true potential of a small group of committed educators and academic leaders to create a more inclusive and transformative educational experience. Wallerstein's thorough investigation of Baruch College's growth, which rigorously taps history, explores politics, and analyzes data on higher education enrollment and finance, is a primer for institutional leaders and an instructive case study for all sectors of higher education given our challenging future."
—**Jillian Kinzie**, associate director, National Survey of Student Engagement, Center for Postsecondary Research, Indiana University Bloomington

"Wallerstein provides a compelling narrative that helps us envision the expansive possibilities of public higher education, even in the context of challenging times. Readers will gain a wealth of practical insights into how Baruch College leveraged a distinctive organizational identity and culture toward financial health and academic innovation."
—**Jay R. Dee**, professor of higher education, University of Massachusetts Boston

Public Higher Education That Works

Public Higher Education That Works

Public Higher Education That Works

One College's Path to Academic Success and Financial Stability

Mitchel B. Wallerstein

TEACHERS COLLEGE PRESS
TEACHERS COLLEGE | COLUMBIA UNIVERSITY
NEW YORK AND LONDON

Published by Teachers College Press,® 1234 Amsterdam Avenue, New York, NY 10027

Copyright © 2024 by Teachers College, Columbia University

Front cover design by Peter Donahue. Photo courtesy of the Office of Communications, Marketing and Public Affairs, Baruch College

All rights reserved. No part of this publication may be reproduced or transmitted in any form or by any means, electronic or mechanical, including photocopy, or any information storage and retrieval system, without permission from the publisher. For reprint permission and other subsidiary rights requests, please contact Teachers College Press, Rights Dept.: tcpressrights@tc.columbia.edu

Library of Congress Cataloging-in-Publication Data

Names: Wallerstein, Mitchel B., author.
Title: Public higher education that works : one college's path to academic success and financial stability / Mitchel B. Wallerstein.
Description: Second edition. | New York : Teachers College Press, [2024] | Includes index. | Summary: "The former college president of Baruch College of The City University of New York details how the institution became a "positive outlier" during a tumultuous time for public higher education"— Provided by publisher.
Identifiers: LCCN 2024012369 (print) | LCCN 2024012370 (ebook) | ISBN 9780807786444 (paper ; acid-free paper) | ISBN 9780807786451 (hardcover; acid-free paper) | ISBN 9780807782767 (ebook)
Subjects: LCSH: City University of New York—History. | Bernard M. Baruch College—History. | Public universities and colleges—United States—Finance. | Public universities and colleges—Curricula—United States.
Classification: LCC LD3835 .W35 2024 (print) | LCC LD3835 (ebook) | DDC 378.747/1—dc23/eng/20240513
LC record available at https://lccn.loc.gov/2024012369
LC ebook record available at https://lccn.loc.gov/2024012370

ISBN 978-0-8077-8644-4 (paper)
ISBN 978-0-8077-8645-1 (hardcover)
ISBN 978-0-8077-8276-7 (ebook)

Printed on acid-free paper
Manufactured in the United States of America

*For Maeve, River, Lucie, Max,
and Cecelia—the lights of my life*

Contents

Preface	xiii
Introduction	**1**
Public Higher Education: A Very Brief History	1
The Uncertain State of Public Higher Education	2
The View From State Capitals	3
Pressure to Keep Tuition Low	4
Public vs. Private Tuition Cost Divergence	5
Enrollment Patterns and Demographics: Public vs. Private	6
1. A Brief History of CUNY and Baruch College and Their Enduring Values and Challenges	**9**
CUNY's Historic Mission: Making Higher Education Affordable and Accessible	11
The New York City Fiscal Crisis	12
The Failed "Open Admissions" Experiment	14
Chronic State Underfunding of CUNY	15
The Upstate vs. Downstate Problem	17
The Complicated Relationship Between CUNY and Its Constituent Colleges	18
2. The Special Character of Baruch and Its Students	**21**
The New York City Tapestry	21
Geographic Distribution	24
Social and Economic Mobility	24

	Academic Focus	28
	International Character	29
	Careers After Graduation	30
	Nature vs. Nurture?	31
3.	**How Does Baruch Compare Nationally?**	**33**
	Academic Quality	33
	Affordability	37
	The Geographic Factor	38
	An Analysis of PHEIs Comparable to Baruch	38
4.	**Challenges Facing Baruch and Other Public Higher Education Institutions**	**43**
	Political Support for Public Higher Education	43
	Addressing the Needs of Students Who Commute and Work	46
	Dealing With a Unionized Faculty and Staff	47
	Dealing With Severe Space Constraints and Aging Facilities	49
	Mobilizing Private Philanthropic Support for a Public Institution	53
5.	**Indicators of Baruch's Success**	**57**
	Increasing Quality of the Student Body	59
	Support for Student Success	60
	New Academic Programs and Initiatives	61
	Increasing the College's Endowment	64
	Developing More Effective Management Tools to Improve Financial Stability	65
	New and Improved Campus Facilities and Outdoor Space	69
	Achieving Strong National and Regional Rankings	70
	Growing National and International Visibility	71
6.	**Does Baruch College Have a "Secret Sauce"?**	**73**
	Baruch's Advantageous Position Within the CUNY System	73
	Does Baruch *Have* a "Secret Sauce"?	81

7.	**Is the Baruch "Model" Sustainable and Replicable?**	83
	What Explains Baruch's Academic Success and Financial Stability?	83
	Can the Baruch College "Model" Be Replicated Elsewhere?	85
	The Future Sustainability of the "Baruch Model"	88
8.	**Reflections on the Future of Public Higher Education**	93
	The Challenges Facing Higher Education in General	93
	The Growing Public vs. Private Cost Gap	95
	Providing an Educated Workforce for the 21st Century	97
	Reimagining the U.S. Higher Education System	97
	Conclusion	98
Endnotes		101
Index		117
About the Author		121

Preface

I had been considering the idea of writing this book for a number of years, particularly as my tenure as president of Baruch College was drawing to a close. I had the honor of leading Baruch for a decade, from 2010 to 2020, and I stepped down in June 2020, right at the height of the COVID-19 pandemic in New York, shortly after my successor, Dr. S. David Wu, was named. I had always felt that there was an important story to tell about the ingredients of Baruch's academic and financial success in the face of challenging times for public higher education. Perhaps for obvious reasons, I ultimately decided to focus on the 10-year period of my presidency, because it is the time frame of which I have firsthand knowledge and because it was a notable era of growth and academic success for the college.

Given the academic quality and professional accomplishments of the Baruch faculty, staff, and students, it has always been something of a mystery to me why Baruch is not better known outside of the New York metropolitan area. Part of the explanation for this may relate to the fact that although the college has been in existence for more than 55 years and has consistently been ranked among the top public colleges in the country (a point that will be discussed extensively in this volume), it is not an independent entity. It is, in fact, a part of the largest public urban university in the United States, The City University of New York (CUNY), which annually enrolls more than 240,000 full-time students on 25 campuses, all of which are located within the boundaries of the city of New York. (Baruch itself has a total enrollment of more than 20,000 students, undergraduate and graduate.) And for reasons that also mystify me, CUNY itself is not very well known outside of the New York metropolitan area.

A second explanation may relate to the fact that, unlike many of the large land-grant universities that are located in other parts of the country, neither Baruch nor CUNY as a whole is an R1 research university. Rather, the university and its constituent colleges are dedicated to the education of tens of thousands of smart, striving young people, many of whom are immigrants and the majority of whom come from economically challenging backgrounds. By enrolling in Baruch, or in one of the other CUNY colleges, students change not only their economic circumstances but also their life trajectories. So it is my hope that this volume will help to increase Baruch's visibility and give the college some of the recognition that I believe it justifiably deserves.

The central question that I will be exploring in the pages that follow is: What accounts for Baruch's success? What has enabled this underfunded, physically constrained college, located in the heart of midtown Manhattan, to prosper and grow and to remain financially stable when so many other public higher education institutions (including some of the other CUNY colleges) have struggled financially and, in some cases, academically? Indeed, just as I was completing this volume, there has been news that several well-known public universities have been forced to make deep budget cuts and to close academic departments or programs. Baruch, on the other hand, is moving in a decidedly different and far more positive direction.

There are many people I need to thank for helping to make this book possible. First and foremost, I want to express my appreciation to Lucina Chavez-Rosique, who served most ably as my research assistant on this project, while also simultaneously pursuing a graduate degree in the Marxe School of Public and International Affairs at Baruch. There was an enormous amount of data and diverse information sources in the higher education sector that needed to be reviewed and analyzed to produce this volume. Lucina helped me to identify these and to organize all of the information. She subsequently made important contributions in helping to determine what information would tell the Baruch story most clearly and effectively. Finally, she prepared the data and organized the tables and charts that appear in the volume.

During the research phase of the project, I received important financial support from the Marxe School of Public and International Affairs in the form of a Marxe Dean's Research Award, which helped to facilitate the collection and analysis of data. (One of the graduate degree programs offered by the Marxe School is Higher Education Administration, and it is my hope that the book will be of use to the graduate students in that program.) I am grateful to Dean Sherry Ryan, to Angelina Delgado, and to the faculty of the Marxe School of Public and International Affairs for making these funds available.

I would like to thank some of the key members of the Baruch College senior professional staff and others at CUNY for their critical assistance in providing, or directing me to, important data and other information that were essential to the development of this volume. Specifically, I want to acknowledge the assistance that I received from Katharine Cobb, Cheryl Dejong, Mary Gorman, Rosa Kelly, Art King, Kenya Lee, David Shanton, Ellen Stein, and Andrew Wallace (of Hunter College). Similarly, I would like to thank Terry Hartle, the now-retired Senior Vice President of the American Council on Education, for his assistance in helping to provide access to important national higher education data. I also wish to acknowledge the important insights and assistance provided by Dr. H. Fenwick Huss, the former dean of the Zicklin School of Business at Baruch; Dr. David Birdsell, the former dean of the Marxe School of Public and International Affairs; and Dr. Jessica Lang, the current dean of the Weissman School of Arts and Sciences, regarding their respective schools' programs and accomplishments.

I asked a number of esteemed, current and former Baruch and CUNY colleagues, as well as outside experts, to review a draft of the manuscript and to offer suggestions for its improvement. I would like to thank, in this regard, Carol Berkin, David Birdsell, Scott Evenbeck, Anne Kirschner, Anthony Knerr, Jessica Lang, Myung-Soo Lee, Clara Lovett, Terrence Martell, and James McCarthy for their important and insightful comments and specific suggestions, which helped me to identify holes in the manuscript, to draw important connections, and to improve the quality and accuracy of the analysis. That said, I alone am responsible for the content and for all the observations made and conclusions reached herein.

Finally, I would like to acknowledge the constant moral and emotional support and patient forbearance of my wife of 50 years, Dr. Susan Perlik, who tolerated my preoccupation during the many months that I was at work on this volume. I could not have completed this book without her loving encouragement and support!

Public Higher Education That Works

Public Higher Education
That Works

Introduction

This is a story about a "little engine that could."[1] It is the story of how one publicly supported institution of higher education managed to overcome serious and continuing financial constraints, physical space limitations, and other obstacles to become highly ranked and nationally recognized, offering a range of degrees from the baccalaureate to the doctorate and graduating tens of thousands of striving individuals, many of whom were the first in their family ever to attend college. I will argue in these pages that Baruch College is, in fact, a *positive outlier* in the world of public higher education; it is an institution that has succeeded where many of its peer institutions have (and, in some cases, continue to) struggle, both financially and academically. I will explore the various factors that have contributed to its success, and in the process, I will attempt to answer the question of whether there is anything unique about Baruch's approach and whether the model can be replicated at other public institutions.

PUBLIC HIGHER EDUCATION: A VERY BRIEF HISTORY

Three U.S. universities lay claim to being the oldest *public* institution of higher education in the country: the University of Georgia, the University of North Carolina, and the College of William & Mary in Virginia.[2] Each has some basis for the claim: The University of Georgia was the first to be established by state charter in 1785; the University of North Carolina was the first to hold classes and graduate students as a *public* institution in 1795; and the College of William & Mary had the oldest founding, in 1693, but it was operated as a private institution for over 200 years, until 1906, when it, too, became a publicly supported institution.[3] The underlying point, of course, is that publicly supported institutions have long played an important role in higher education in the United States.

With the passage of the Morrill Act of 1862, the United States initiated a unique system of federal support for higher education, specifically in agriculture and "the mechanical arts."[4] The national system of "land-grant" universities and colleges has expanded over the years to include institutions in all 50 states, the District of Columbia, and U.S. territories.[5] Today, the majority are known simply as "state universities," and they receive millions of dollars in direct support each year from their home state and from the federal government. Known for their excellence in teaching, research, and extension, the institutions make up the land-grant system, and they are widely admired and emulated around the world.

Many of these large state universities have acquired substantial endowment resources over the years since their founding. There are, in fact, at least 50 public higher education institutions (known hereafter as PHEIs), more than 30 of which are single-campus institutions, with endowments of $1 billion or more.[6] Schools like The University of Texas, the University of Michigan, and the University of Virginia are representative of this category. These institutions are almost all R1 research universities, and they typically have ample resources to provide student support services and financial aid that are the equal of many of the top private colleges and universities. As a result, many of them report undergraduate completion rates that approach or exceed 90%. For obvious reasons, these well-resourced PHEIs do not represent a useful peer reference group for this analysis.[7]

At the other end of the financial spectrum are the many PHEIs throughout the country that have only modest endowments—or, in some cases, very little endowment at all. These universities are primarily teaching institutions, and they generally educate a different type of student—typically, young people coming from underprivileged backgrounds with extremely limited family resources and/or students who may be paying their own way through college. It is within this universe of PHEIs that Baruch College, and the entire CUNY system, is situated.[8]

THE UNCERTAIN STATE OF PUBLIC HIGHER EDUCATION

Public higher education institutions have awarded hundreds of thousands of undergraduate and graduate degrees over the years; they produced important research accomplishments (including work that subsequently resulted in Nobel Prizes); and they enabled people from economically disadvantaged backgrounds who otherwise could not have afforded to pursue a college degree to achieve their dreams. But many of these institutions are now under serious financial and academic stress. *Financial* stress results directly from the fact that budgets for higher education in many states have been mostly flat—and, in some cases, have actually declined in real terms—for at least the past decade, or longer in some cases. *Academic* stress often is a direct corollary of inadequate public support, and there are some prominent recent examples where PHEIs have been forced to cut departments, programs, and faculty.[9] There are other kinds of "academic stresses," of course, including those that result from political pressure brought to bear on public institutions by governors, state legislatures, or in some cases, by outside groups either promoting or opposing certain controversial issues.[10]

Unlike private higher education institutions, which often can rely on substantial endowments and their ability to mount large and successful fundraising campaigns and to raise tuition to cope with economic downturns and meet urgent needs, most PHEIs do not, with some notable exceptions,[11] possess large endowments or have the ability (or desire) to continuously raise tuition. So, when state governments reduce or flatline their operating budgets, or when states provide budget increases that do not keep pace with inflation, the impacts on the universities can often be serious and long-lasting.

During the period immediately following the Great Recession (2009–2010), for example, serious shortfalls in tax revenue forced the state of New York (along with many other states) to make significant and sudden midyear reductions in the operating budgets of many government agencies, including both of the state-funded university systems, CUNY and the State University of New York (SUNY). (I happened to be in my first year as president of Baruch College at that time, and I was forced to make difficult and very painful decisions, right in the middle of an academic year, regarding how to cope with the sudden elimination of millions of dollars of operating support.)

In CUNY's case, increases in state budget support have often seemed to be provided only grudgingly. In 1976, at the height of the New York City financial crisis, a deal was struck between the city and the state to move financial responsibility for CUNY's so-called "senior colleges" (of which Baruch is one) to the state budget.[12] Rarely a priority for most New York governors since that time, CUNY typically has received only very modest (and sometimes effectively no) annual budget increases, despite the fact that (a) its student population has continued to increase,[13] (b) the majority of CUNY graduates remain in the New York City metropolitan area and contribute to state and local tax revenues, and (c) New York City generates a disproportionately larger share of state tax revenue than does the upstate region of New York.

THE VIEW FROM STATE CAPITALS

Some states are, of course, in better financial condition than others and are therefore better able to provide reliable, continuing support for public higher education. Texas, with its oil revenue and strong economy, offers a good example. But in an era when enrollments are generally flat or declining, especially at community colleges, as a result of demographic trends and a volatile economy, even the better-off states may not see increasing support for PHEIs as a high priority. As a result, even when states have budget surpluses, there is no guarantee of a funding boost for public educational institutions.

Support for public higher education also must compete with dozens of other pressing public needs at the state level, including housing, health care, primary and secondary education, road construction and repair, other infrastructure construction and repair, and job creation programs—just to name a few. In addition, especially in years of budget surplus, there is often political pressure for the implementation of tax cuts or the placement of excess funds into a "rainy-day fund." And if the decision is to cut taxes, this only increases the likelihood that future economic downturns that result in reduced tax revenues can force states to enact deep cuts in order to balance their budgets.[14] Public higher education is often a victim when this occurs, and as previously noted, this is precisely what happened in New York on several previous occasions at both CUNY and SUNY.

PRESSURE TO KEEP TUITION LOW

The historical mission of Baruch College and The City University of New York, like its predecessor, the Free Academy, has traditionally been to educate the students of the city of New York (and beyond), and the university's natural target audience was—and continues to be—the children of the millions of predominantly immigrant families who have continued to flock to New York for more than a century in search of a better life. But most of these families have only very limited ability to pay for the education of their children, and many live at or below the poverty line. Until the New York City financial crisis of the 1970s, the CUNY colleges were essentially free; students paid only a modest fee and for the purchase of their books, which they could buy used and then trade back in.

Even after free tuition was ended, due to the city's financial crisis, the cost of attending CUNY remained extremely low in comparison to other PHEIs across the country. And while CUNY tuition has slowly increased over time, the state of New York has been able to offset most of the increase for financially eligible students through the Tuition Assistance Program (TAP), which was established in 1974 and which has been adjusted periodically since CUNY started charging tuition. Families must have a total income under $100,000 to qualify for the scholarship assistance, which can be used at any public or private higher education institution in the state. This means that those students who qualify financially can still attend CUNY schools, like Baruch, essentially tuition-free.

Unfortunately, however, this situation applies *only* to those students whose families meet the income threshold. For students from families that do not qualify, the overall cost of attending a CUNY college has continued to increase, though the university remains a fantastic economic deal, with one of the lowest annual tuition rates in the country. Nevertheless, whenever the state approves an increase in tuition, there is always a vocal outcry from those who argue either that public higher education institutions should be free for everyone, or that tuition charges should at the very least be frozen at current levels and not increased further.

Both versions of the argument proceed from the politically unrealistic and economically nonviable assumption that state legislators and the governor can somehow be convinced to find the funds to substantially increase annual support for public higher education in order to make this happen. But, as previously noted, there really is no basis to believe that such a major increase in public support will be forthcoming anytime in the foreseeable future. Thus, the likelihood of making CUNY (and, presumably, SUNY) once again tuition-free is effectively zero. In fact, it is quite possible that there could and will be further reductions in state support in the coming years, particularly if state tax revenues should shrink for any reason, and this, in turn, could necessitate further tuition increases.

PUBLIC VS. PRIVATE TUITION COST DIVERGENCE

One of the most striking features of higher education during the first 3 decades of the 21st century has been the growing divergence between the cost of public versus private higher education. As indicated in Table I.1, the average cost (tuition and fees only) for public higher education institutions, nationwide, has risen from $3,501 per year in 2000 to $9,375 per year in 2020. This is as compared with the average cost of private higher education during this same time period, which increased from $15,810 per year in 2000 to $35,850 per year in 2020. Clearly, this cost divergence between public and private, just for tuition and fees, has been dramatic; and if all of the other major expenses (i.e., room and board,[15] books, transportation, and other living) are also included, the contrast is even greater.

This growing public-private cost divergence is having an especially serious impact on middle-class families, who might previously have aspired to send their children to a private college or university but who are finding themselves effectively priced out. While private institutions have done their best to remain affordable, either by heavily discounting their

Table I.1. The Cost of Tuition and Fees: Public vs. Private Colleges and Universities, 2000–2020

Source: U.S. Department of Education, National Center for Education Statistics, Integrated Postsecondary Education Data System (IPEDS) Fall Enrollment, 2000–2020

tuition or by reaching more aggressively into their endowments (assuming they have one) to offer additional financial aid, they face significant limits in using either strategy without threatening their financial solvency. As a result, many families ultimately decide to send their children to public institutions, where they believe they can get a quality education *without* saddling either the parents or the student, or some combination, with a significant amount of debt.

ENROLLMENT PATTERNS AND DEMOGRAPHICS: PUBLIC VS. PRIVATE

The growing divergence between the cost of public versus private universities and colleges is evident in the enrollment patterns and the demographic makeup of the students who typically attend the two different types of educational institutions. It has always been the case that students from families with more limited means have tended to opt for publicly funded institutions where tuition and most other costs are lower. As previously noted, private institutions—at least those with significant endowments—have tried to achieve their goals for economic, racial, ethnic, and gender diversity in their entering classes by offering generous financial aid and/or by deeply discounting tuition.[16] But despite these efforts, publicly funded universities and colleges remain the destination of choice for the majority of underrepresented minority students, especially those from low-income families, as well as those from more affluent families who do not qualify for as much (or sometimes any) state and federal assistance.

All of the aforementioned issues will be explored in the chapters that follow in an attempt to explain what has enabled one PHEI, Baruch College, to succeed and prosper when many of its peer institutions have struggled. In the first chapter, I briefly review the unusual history of CUNY and Baruch College. In succeeding chapters, I examine how Baruch compares on a national basis to a group of 14 reference peer institutions and the challenges that all of these public institutions face. After exploring various specific indicators of Baruch's success, I consider directly whether the college's success can be attributed to a specific plan or special approach, whether the "Baruch model" is sustainable over the long term, and whether the "Baruch model" is replicable in other institutional settings and states. The volume concludes with some reflections on the future of *public* higher education and why it is needed now more than ever.

CHAPTER 1

A Brief History of CUNY and Baruch College and Their Enduring Values and Challenges

The City University of New York (CUNY) and Baruch College share a unique history and legacy. The building that served for many years as the original location of Baruch College, at the corner of Lexington Avenue and 23rd Street in Manhattan, was previously the site of the Free Academy, which was the antecedent to the modern-day CUNY. The importance of Free Academy as a model for CUNY (and, by implication, for Baruch) cannot be overemphasized.[1]

The Free Academy was established in the middle of the 19th century when immigrants were pouring into the United States, especially from Europe. New York City's population had grown to more than 500,000 and many people were newly arrived. But higher education was generally available only to the affluent, so a plan was developed to educate and train New Yorkers of all backgrounds and classes without regard to their financial circumstances because there was no requirement for them to pay tuition. The motivation for this unprecedented initiative was visionary and forward-looking: It recognized that the city's continued growth and prosperity depended on the broad availability of an educated workforce, and education was something that most of the new arrivals lacked.

The New York State legislature formally acted to establish the Free Academy in 1847. In a letter published in *The Morning Courier and New York Enquirer* on March 15, 1847, Townsend Harris, then the president of New York City's Board of Education, stated in reference to this event, "Make them the property of the people—open the doors to all—let the children of the rich and the poor take their seats together and know of no distinction save that of industry, good conduct and intellect."[2] And Dr. Horace Webster, the first president of the Free Academy when it opened on January 21, 1849, stated, "The experiment is to be tried, whether the children of the people, the children of the whole people, can be educated; and whether an institution of the highest grade, can be successfully controlled by the popular will, not by the privileged few."[3]

Figure 1.1. An Artist's Rendering of the Free Academy as It Appeared at the Time of Its Opening in 1849

These sentiments were quite revolutionary, especially for that era. As noted, higher education at the time was typically accessible only to the wealthy elite, not to the working class. So the tuition-free status of the Free Academy made it possible for those of lower economic status to pursue a college education as well. But also embedded in the statements by Harris and Webster was another important idea—namely, an *egalitarian* vision for higher education in which rich and poor students would be educated side by side. This core value has been carried down to the present day in CUNY, more than 175 years after the founding of the Free Academy. And it has enduring value and relevance for higher education in the 21st century. At Baruch, these values are even inscribed permanently on the wall outside of the Office of Student Affairs.

In 1866, the Free Academy, which was a male-only institution, was renamed the College of the City of New York, and it later became known as the City College of New York (CCNY). Over the ensuing years, when many private colleges and universities were admitting only the children of the white Protestant establishment, thousands of bright individuals (including especially, many Jewish students) attended City College, because they were unable to gain admission to these other colleges and universities and because they could not afford to pay private school tuition. The academic excellence and status of City College as a working-class school earned it many sobriquets, including "the Harvard of the Proletariat," "the poor man's Harvard," and "Harvard-on-the-Hudson."[4] Ten CCNY graduates ultimately went on to win Nobel Prizes. Like CUNY students today, they were the children of immigrants and the working class, and often the first in their families to go to college.

The precursor to the present-day Baruch College was established in 1919 as City College's School of Business and Civic Administration on the site of the previous Free Academy.[5] The school was renamed in 1953 in honor of Bernard M. Baruch—financier (and first Jewish member of the New York Stock Exchange), statesman, adviser to multiple presidents, devoted CCNY alumnus, and the first donor to the college. In 1968, Baruch became a separate, independent senior college in the CUNY system. In retrospect, it might not have been possible to establish a new independent campus with such an initially narrow mission (i.e., business and government) anyplace *other* than in New York City, given the size of the business and government communities located there and the resulting demand for its graduates.[6]

The City University of New York itself was officially established in 1961, during the administration of Governor Nelson A. Rockefeller, initially by combining into one university CCNY, Hunter College, Brooklyn College, Queens College, and five community colleges.[7] Today, CUNY is the largest, urban, public university system in the United States, consisting of 25 campuses with more than 240,000 enrolled degree-seeking students.

CUNY'S HISTORIC MISSION: MAKING HIGHER EDUCATION AFFORDABLE AND ACCESSIBLE

As noted above, CUNY has continued the long tradition of making higher education affordable and accessible for tens of thousands of students from the city of New York (and New York State), including many whose family economic circumstances would not otherwise enable them to pursue higher education. Indeed, this has long been the university's principal mission: to provide a quality education to all students, regardless of means or background.[8] Today, 65% of Baruch students,[9] and 50% of CUNY students overall,[10] come from families living at or below the poverty line.

The end of World War II and the passage of the G.I. Bill fueled an enormous enrollment boom in New York and across the country. Returning G.I.s sought to reenter the peacetime economy, starting or resuming educational pursuits that they had put on hold during the war. In addition, a growing number of women were enrolled. Many had held wartime jobs while the men were away fighting and then had subsequently given up— or lost—their employment at the war's end when the men returned. As a result, co-education was instituted at City College (previously all male) and Hunter College (previously all female) beginning in 1951. For many years after the end of World War II, the colleges that would later become part of CUNY continued the longstanding tradition of *free* undergraduate tuition—students paid only for their books and a modest processing fee. But this policy did not last; it simply was not financially sustainable because public support for higher education failed to keep pace after the war with the enormous increase in enrollments and the cost of operating a growing number of campuses.

THE NEW YORK CITY FISCAL CRISIS

The precipitating event that actually marked the end of free college tuition at CUNY was the fiscal crisis that engulfed New York City in 1975. In that year, the banks reviewed the city's revenue projections and decided they were no longer adequate to underwrite its notes and bonds and other financial obligations. U.S. economic stagnation in the 1970s had hit the city particularly hard, and this was amplified by a large movement of middle-class residents to the suburbs, which drained the city of tax revenue. As a result, New York could no longer borrow sufficient money to operate, and it was literally running out of funds to meet payrolls and operate programs. In short, it faced the real prospect of having to declare bankruptcy.

In response, the state of New York created the Municipal Assistance Corporation (MAC), which was composed of eight prominent bankers. Under the leadership of Felix G. Rohatyn, the chairman of the Lazard investment firm, the MAC eventually proposed a series of draconian fiscal measures for New York City, which included a wage freeze, major layoffs, a subway fare increase, and the initiation of tuition at CUNY. The New York State Legislature supported the MAC by passing a law converting both the city sales tax and stock transfer tax into state taxes, which when collected were then used as security for the MAC bonds. The state of New York also passed a state law that created an Emergency Financial Control Board to monitor the city's finances, required the city to balance its budget within 3 years, and directed the city to follow accepted accounting practices.[11]

In fall 1976, the free tuition policy was officially ended, and the state of New York took over the funding of CUNY's five senior colleges, of which Baruch was by then one. Financial responsibility for the CUNY community colleges and the so-called "comprehensive colleges"[12] remained, however, the responsibility of the city of New York. Modest tuition charges were instituted at all of the CUNY colleges, just as had already been done at the schools that were part of the SUNY system. Meanwhile, CUNY students were added to the state's need-based Tuition Assistance Program (TAP), which had been created initially to assist and encourage private colleges to accept financially needy students. Full-time students who met the income eligibility criteria were able to receive TAP support, ensuring for the first time that financial hardship would not deprive CUNY students of a college education.[13]

This bifurcated financial support arrangement, with New York State and New York City each responsible for providing part of the university's funding, was, if nothing else, unique. But it also has proven over the years to be problematic. First, some governors have tended to favor larger increases in operating and capital support for SUNY.[14] This often resulted either in flat budgets, or only very modest increases, for the CUNY system, increases that did not come close to keeping pace with operating costs or with the rate of inflation. This meant that CUNY was forced to absorb the increased costs, which effectively reduced its net operating funds.

In some years, during and immediately following the Great Recession of 2008–2009, for example, the budgets for *both* CUNY and SUNY were cut significantly. At Baruch and on the other CUNY campuses, the impact was immediate; virtually all discretionary spending was eliminated, basic maintenance of facilities deteriorated because part-time custodial employees were laid off, basic supplies became unavailable, and multiple academic and staff searches were suspended. Yet another result of these budget cuts was increased reliance on adjunct faculty and an increase in average class sizes.

Second, the divided financial support between the city and the state has meant that CUNY is scrutinized by and must strike deals with *both* government entities for each fiscal year. Third, some governors—Andrew Cuomo, in particular, comes to mind—have bridled at the fact that, due to the bifurcated financial and political responsibility, they did not have complete control of the CUNY board of trustees and its policy decisions. Under an agreement reached between the state and the city, two-thirds of CUNY's board is appointed by the governor and one-third by the mayor. This arrangement also has meant that the members of the CUNY board have divided loyalties, and the university chancellery must serve two masters simultaneously.[15]

The net result of these factors, taken together, has been that CUNY's ability to develop new academic programs, to hire and/or replace faculty, and to renovate facilities or build new ones has at times been severely constrained. This has, in turn, hampered the university's ability to maintain academic quality and match past success. Many of CUNY's academic buildings, for example, are more than 100 years old; they are physically worn out and technologically obsolete. Moreover, these facilities were never designed to handle the current volume of students (240,000) attending day and evening classes—and in some cases, 7-days-per-week operation.

THE FAILED "OPEN ADMISSIONS" EXPERIMENT

Under the policy of "open admissions" at CUNY, most formal requirements for admission were eliminated and every New York City high school graduate was guaranteed a seat at a CUNY college without consideration of their high school grade point average or SAT scores. The policy was developed in the context of the societal and political upheavals of the 1960s, which included the assassination of Dr. Martin Luther King, Jr. and the resulting urban riots. There were numerous campus protests at CUNY during that period, which included a number of building takeovers, to protest the war in Vietnam and other social issues.

The major grievance expressed by Black and Latino students concerned their significant *underrepresentation* in the city's public institution of higher education. Minorities at that time represented 40% of New York City's high school students, but whites occupied 87% of the seats at the senior colleges and 68% in community colleges.[16] As Stephen Steinberg has noted, the New York City Board of Higher Education (which was the precursor to the CUNY Board of Trustees) expressed a commitment as early as 1964 to "expand opportunities for poorer minority students" and approved plans—that were to be phased in between 1971 to 1975—for an open admissions program that would guarantee every high school graduate a seat in a community college.[17] But the 1969 student strikes led the board, under pressure from the John Lindsay mayoral administration, to precipitously accelerate the launch of open admissions in the fall of 1970, while at the same time assuring that all entering students would have access to remedial courses and other necessary support services.[18]

While it can be argued that the underlying goal of open admissions—namely, to broaden access to CUNY by people of color—was both laudable and entirely in keeping with the historic mission of the institution to educate "all of the people" of the city of New York, the reality of its implementation was substantially different. The policy did initially result in a doubling of overall admissions to CUNY and a *tripling* of African American and Hispanic admissions, but the lack of even minimum admission standards meant that many of the students who enrolled were seriously deficient in their secondary school education and therefore unprepared for the rigors of higher education. As a result, many failed their courses, and a large number subsequently dropped out. The policy also had a devastating impact on the faculties of the CUNY senior colleges—most notably, at the flagship City College of New York. Some of the most able faculty either retired or departed for positions elsewhere out of frustration.

Unfortunately, the imposition of a modest tuition charge in 1976 and the reinstatement of academic requirements for admission to the CUNY senior colleges resulted in a significant decline in the number of minority enrollees at CUNY, even though the open admissions policy officially remained in place for another 22 years. Ultimately, in 1998, former Congressman and Bronx Borough president Herman Badillo, who was then serving as the chair of the CUNY Board of Trustees, sponsored a resolution to phase out remedial courses at the CUNY senior colleges. And a few months later, then New York Mayor Rudolph Giuliani impaneled a task force, which was chaired by the former president of Yale University, Benno Schmidt Jr., to undertake a sweeping review of CUNY.

The Schmidt panel subsequently issued an influential and widely read report, which was titled *The City University of New York: An Institution Adrift*. The report described CUNY as "moribund" and in "a spiral of decline." It urged CUNY to "reinvent" open admissions with "the placement of the remediation function in the community colleges"; it also recommended that CUNY should become a fully integrated university system, rather than a confederation of independent colleges.[19] The report led, among other things, to a systemwide overhaul of admissions that formally ended the open admissions experiment. In retrospect, a policy that had been initiated with the best of intentions ultimately resulted in serious damage to the reputation and academic quality of the CUNY senior colleges and to the university as a whole (and to many of its enrolled students), as well as to its ability to recruit and retain high-quality faculty.

The negative impacts of the open admissions experiment continued to be felt for many years, even after the policy had been officially ended. Baruch College was fortunate, in this regard, because it managed to largely escape these negative impacts. Even to this day, there is speculation about how and why Baruch managed to avoid the fate that befell CCNY and some of the other senior colleges. Most think it was due to the fact that standards for admission to the Baruch business school were never eliminated. So, for example, the calculus requirement was maintained even during the years of open enrollment. This helped to maintain the overall rigor and quality of the Baruch degree and of the students admitted to the program.[20]

Benno Schmidt subsequently became chair of the CUNY Board of Trustees in 2003 and remained in that position for the next 13 years. Under Schmidt's leadership, and that of CUNY Chancellor Matthew Goldstein, who was appointed in 1999, the university slowly moved in a new direction, one that implemented the major recommendations of the Schmidt panel and moved the institution back closer to its historic mission.

CHRONIC STATE UNDERFUNDING OF CUNY

Since the New York City financial crisis of the 1970s, the state of New York has provided, on average, about 52% of the university's annual

Table 1.1. New York State Budget Support for CUNY, 2010–2020

SUPPORT FROM STATE OF NY
2010–2020 (IN THOUSANDS)

Source: OpenBudget.NYS.org/BudgetActuals/2023–2024HigherEducation/CityUniversityofNewYork. https://openbudget.ny.gov/spendingForm.html

operating budget.[21] And depending on the governor in power and their relationship with the New York City political establishment, CUNY has often faced a serious challenge to obtain adequate state support. Table 1.1 summarizes the annual budget support provided by the state of New York between fiscal year (FY) 2010 and FY 2020. The table reveals that, while the state budget for CUNY did increase over the 10-year period, it was essentially flat when adjusted for inflation, and it failed to provide the university with sufficient resources to deal with the very substantial student population growth that it experienced during the decade or address its deferred maintenance needs.

Some governors have taken the position that now, many decades since the New York City financial crisis, the city should be doing more to support CUNY (which does bear its name, after all). There is some logic to this argument—except for the fact that realistically it would be all but impossible, from a financial standpoint, for New York City to come up with the additional $4 billion in annual budget resources to replace the funding provided by the state. Moreover, this money would need to be *in addition* to the annual support that the city already provides for the seven community colleges that are part of the CUNY system.

During the final years of Governor Andrew Cuomo's tenure, he floated a trial balloon suggesting that the state should end its financial support for CUNY altogether and return the financial responsibility once again to the city of New York.[22] While it is doubtful that this was ever a serious proposal, it did indicate that, at least in Cuomo's mind, CUNY was an unwelcome "burden." Curiously, however, at another point soon thereafter, the Governor floated an entirely *different* trial balloon, proposing to merge CUNY and SUNY.[23]

This idea, too, was never apparently serious or likely to be implemented. In reality, it would have created the largest public university in the United States (and one of the largest in the world), with more than 80 campuses statewide! Even a cursory look at the administrative and logistical challenges involved in establishing, integrating, and managing an 80-campus university system scattered across a state the size of New York makes evident why such a merger would be a nonstarter.

THE UPSTATE VS. DOWNSTATE PROBLEM

The underlying problem in connection with the size and reliability of state support for CUNY is often characterized as the "upstate vs. downstate" problem—meaning the divergence of political and economic interests between those living in different geographic areas, especially in a state like New York where there are great disparities in wealth and job availability between the regions. That said, New York is similar to a number of other states that also have an upstate-downstate divide.

By informal agreement, SUNY maintains only a limited presence in New York City,[24] and CUNY does not operate beyond the five boroughs. The inevitable result of this division of labor is that political support for SUNY is primarily located upstate, whereas support for CUNY lies in the downstate, New York City metropolitan area. Because there are fewer New York City representatives in Albany, and because many sitting governors have often been more interested in currying political support with upstate voters where the SUNY campuses are located,[25] CUNY frequently has gotten shortchanged in the final budget reconciliation process.

There is no easy resolution to this problem, which has existed for many decades. Those representing the upstate interests argue that the New York City area is disproportionately wealthier than the upstate cities and towns, which have seen a serious outflow of manufacturing and other jobs, and that the upstate region therefore deserves a larger share of state resources. But social and economic demands on the downstate region are considerable as well, especially given the continuing inflow of immigrant and refugee populations. In truth, *both* CUNY and SUNY are serving economically disadvantaged student populations, which to some degree neutralizes this argument from the standpoint of budgetary allocations. But it is also the case that the SUNY system is considerably larger than CUNY (SUNY has 64 campuses versus 25 at CUNY), so it is not unreasonable that SUNY would receive the bulk of state higher education resources.

THE COMPLICATED RELATIONSHIP BETWEEN CUNY AND ITS CONSTITUENT COLLEGES

The City University of New York is unique in another way. It operates 25 campuses across the five boroughs of New York City, with all of the colleges within 15 miles of one another. Unlike the PHEIs in other states, which are typically spread across a much larger geographic area (think of the University of California or The University of Texas systems, for example), the unusually close proximity of the CUNY colleges offers the possibility for centralized management to an unprecedented degree. And this is, in fact, the case with regard to labor matters, where faculty and staff contracts are negotiated centrally between the CUNY Chancellery and the Professional Staff Congress[26] (subject to approval by the state and the city). Other functions that are controlled centrally include the negotiation of annual university budgets, which are negotiated between the chancellery and the state and city governments, and the appointment (and tenure) of faculty and senior academic administrators, which must be reviewed and approved by the CUNY Board of Trustees.

Beyond these important functions, however, the CUNY colleges and their faculties still retain some ability for autonomous decision-making. But the colleges are each quite different in terms of their history, campus culture, geographic locations, stated missions, and endowment resources. These differences are reflected in their academic quality, enrollments, and financial performance. Baruch is fortunate, in this regard, to have benefited from its prior connection to City College during its heyday (prior to open admissions), from its location in lower midtown Manhattan, and from its strong academic reputation derived largely from a prestigious business school. As described in detail in the next chapter, Baruch has consistently attracted high-performing students and generated alumni loyalty that has enabled it to raise substantial amounts of private funding on an annual basis. Even during periods when the university has struggled (e.g., during and immediately following the Great Recession and during and after the COVID-19 pandemic), Baruch's application and enrollment numbers remained strong, and therefore, its financial profile also remained positive and stable.

For all these reasons, the CUNY Chancellery has sometimes given Baruch a bit more operating room than some other CUNY colleges, which have struggled with declining enrollments and poor graduation rates that have led, in some cases, to serious financial difficulties. But, although Baruch may be afforded somewhat greater latitude to develop new programs and initiatives, it has rarely been provided with additional *budget* resources to accomplish such objectives. In fact, there was a point during my presidency when we discovered that Baruch was actually cross-subsidizing the rest of CUNY in terms of the allocation of tuition dollars!

Over the years, Baruch has sought to build on its strengths and its academic reputation by developing various curricular and cocurricular programs to enrich and accelerate the learning of its students. A prime example of these special curricular initiatives was the Great Works of Literature program, which was formally a part of the Baruch curriculum until 2013 when CUNY implemented the Pathways initiative.[27] Under the Great Works program, *all* Baruch undergraduates were required to take at least one semester of Great Works of Literature, either in the English Department or in the Department of Modern Languages. The goal of these courses was to set major literary works in their social, historical, religious, economic, and political contexts, while covering a global range of cultures.

Thanks to a strong effort by dedicated Baruch faculty, the major elements of the Great Works program were saved, despite the decision by CUNY to require curricular uniformity across the university. The Baruch department chairs worked closely together and ultimately settled on an option developed by the Zicklin School of Business to require the Great Works program and a liberal arts minor of each undergraduate. Thus, Great Works now resides in what is known as the "College Option" of Pathways, and it is required of the vast majority of Baruch students. Prior to Pathways, however, all the college's undergraduate students had to take Great Works as part of the common core. So while it is the case that Pathways eliminated Great Works from the general curriculum, a modified version was retained through a concerted and collaborative effort by the Baruch faculty.[28,29]

The conflict over the adoption of the Pathways curriculum offers a revealing insight into the struggle with which Baruch has often had to engage to pursue and protect its academic interests. There is a natural tendency in any large university—and CUNY system is one of the largest in the United States—to seek to impose uniformity across all campuses offering the same academic degrees and teaching the same (or similar) curriculum. To a certain extent, this does make sense as a way of assuring that a given degree is of the same quality and content no matter where it is offered. But when the constituent campuses themselves vary dramatically in quality, such a policy has two immediate effects: (1) it tends to drive academic programs—and the colleges themselves—to a lowest common denominator, and (2) it stifles and may actively deter intellectual creativity and innovation. As noted, in Baruch's case, it almost forced the college to sacrifice a well-designed, effective, and popular program (i.e.,

Great Works) because it could not be accommodated within a standardized curriculum. And this is just one example among many.

The negative impact of imposed uniformity can be even more extensive and counterproductive, however, if, as in the case of CUNY, it proceeds from an underlying philosophical approach that all of the constituent elements of the university are—and must be treated as—equal. CUNY has long maintained the pretense that there is no qualitative difference among the 25 colleges that make up the university system, despite *substantial* academic and financial evidence to the contrary. As a result, there is an implicit expectation that all of the colleges will operate more or less in the same fashion, even if some have the capacity and the desire to develop new programs or to set different and higher standards. This unwillingness to recognize and reward quality and to encourage innovation—basically, to accept that there *is* differentiation among the colleges—can be and is a clear impediment to the advancement of the individual colleges and to CUNY as a whole.

CUNY urgently needs to abandon this long-held approach. It must demonstrate a willingness to tolerate and even encourage differentiation. This is the only way that the university can advance and further improve its national standing and reputation. Consider the University of California (UC) system, for example, where Berkeley, UCLA, and San Diego are generally recognized as the "flagship" campuses and are acknowledged as such by the UC system. These flagship schools are given greater latitude—and financial incentives—to innovate, to further improve their quality, and to develop their national reputations. Similarly, within SUNY, Buffalo, Stony Brook, Binghamton, and Albany are recognized as the leading academic elements within the enormous 64-campus system, and they too are treated accordingly.

Under the leadership of the current CUNY chancellor, Dr. Félix Matos Rodriguez, who served previously as the president of Hostos Community College and later Queens College within the CUNY system, there has been some momentum to reform CUNY's management philosophy. But overcoming inertia, built-in bias, and fixed ways of thinking engrained in the system over so many decades continues to be a serious and difficult challenge. It is high time, however, that CUNY adopted an *explicit* policy of differentiation, much like that employed in most other large, public university systems. Such a policy change will unleash the creativity and entrepreneurial potential that exists within the institution's faculty and administrators.

CHAPTER 2

The Special Character of Baruch and Its Students

There can be little doubt that an important factor in Baruch's long-term success is the fierce determination of its students to succeed. While this is surely not a characteristic that is unique to Baruch, there are a variety of reasons why it is a common denominator at the college. The majority of Baruch's highly diverse undergraduate students come from economically disadvantaged backgrounds, and they are working either part- or full-time (while attending school full-time) to pay their way through college and to help support their families. Many are the first in their family to attend college. In 2020, more than 40% of Baruch undergraduates were first-time college attenders.[1]

THE NEW YORK CITY TAPESTRY

Given the enormous racial, ethnic, and cultural diversity of the city of New York, it is hardly surprising that CUNY, and its constituent colleges, are themselves similarly diverse. In light of the large number of first-generation immigrant families who reside in New York, many of whom have total family income that places them near or below the poverty line, CUNY is their *only* viable option, since they cannot afford the cost of sending a child away to school. A strong indicator of this socioeconomic profile is that 61% of Baruch students are Pell Grant[2] recipients,[3] which is one of the highest Pell Grant percentages among all colleges and universities in the country. The combination of extremely low in-state tuition; the state's Tuition Assistance Program (TAP), which is entirely need-based; and the availability of Pell Grants has enabled hundreds of thousands of low-income students to pursue an undergraduate education that likely would have been much less accessible if CUNY did not exist. In most cases, Baruch students live at home, travel to school by subway or bus, and work either part- or full-time while also taking a full course load.

Baruch College is today a highly diverse institution. In 2020, Asian Americans made up the largest percentage of officially designated minority students, representing 41% of the total undergraduate student body. Hispanic students were the 2nd-largest cohort at 25%, and African American students comprised about 9% of the student body.[4] (Baruch was recently designated by the U.S. Department of Education as a "Hispanic-Serving Institution.") As indicated in Table 2.1, these numbers increased during the period of 2010–2020, while the number of white students remained essentially the same. The college has struggled to further increase the number of African American applicants admitted as first-year students.[5]

What these data do not reveal is that a significant number of CUNY and Baruch students are not U.S. citizens. CUNY has long maintained a "don't ask, don't tell" policy regarding undocumented applicants. As a result, specific official numbers do not exist; but a reasonable "guestimate" is that there may be more than 6,000 undocumented students overall in the CUNY system—and of that total, there may be somewhere around a thousand undocumented students studying at Baruch.

Table 2.1. Baruch Enrollment Trends by Race and Ethnicity, 2010-2020

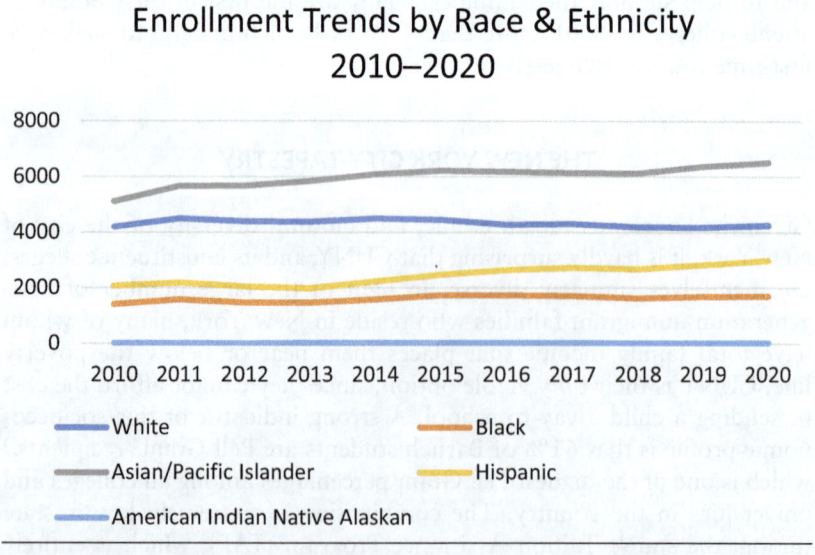

Enrollment Trends by Race & Ethnicity 2010–2020

Year	White	Black	Asian/Pacific Islander	Hispanic	American Indian Native Alaskan
2010	~4200	~1400	~5200	~1900	~0
2011	~4500	~1500	~5600	~2100	~0
2012	~4400	~1400	~5600	~2000	~0
2013	~4400	~1400	~5600	~2000	~0
2014	~4400	~1500	~5800	~2200	~0
2015	~4400	~1500	~6000	~2400	~0
2016	~4300	~1500	~6000	~2400	~0
2017	~4300	~1500	~6100	~2500	~0
2018	~4300	~1500	~6200	~2600	~0
2019	~4300	~1600	~6300	~2800	~0
2020	~4200	~1600	~6400	~2900	~0

Source: Office of Applied Research, Evaluation and Data Analytics, as reflected in the Student Data Book: https://urldefense.proofpoint.com/v2/url?u=https-3A_ _public.tableau.com_app_profile_oira.cuny_viz_StudentDataBook_Enrollment&d =DwMFaQ&c=dTXc8cCP8suVpClwB1HRHQACHN4UFMgL7MtSjCbKyts&r =9HV09kXmkMupgx68eA27AZukpBvjzNF-5Sc4--NbNAzQ67QdTa0gMYKaw acjxYHj&m=lW0g5lJuXY5B-fhaE67Bt2x84WvHR2jakyCir0XKyLkVUDJ8Th _UtGrWuLsliaIp&s=Nvae6WFnWLWFu88itq96xwT_GLpJbk7v-62Z-zBdhdw&e=

CUNY was not always as diverse as it is today, despite its origins as the Free Academy. The desire to increase minority admissions was, in fact, one of the principal motivating factors in CUNY's open admissions policy in the 1970s and 1980s, as described in the previous chapter. A legitimate argument was (and still can be) made that many underrepresented minority students were being denied admission to CUNY because of their inadequate secondary school education, which did not enable them to meet Baruch's admissions standards in terms of grade point average or comprehensive test scores. But it turned out that the failure of the open admissions policy also demonstrated the folly of admitting ill-prepared students, which only set them up for subsequent failure, and made clear that there were better ways to go about addressing this problem.

Baruch College, too, was not as diverse an institution in earlier decades, though not because of any explicit policy of exclusion. As noted in Chapter 1, after World War II there was a significant amount of anti-Semitism in higher education that lasted well into the 1970s.[6] Well-qualified Jewish students either were denied admission to elite Ivy League and other private universities and colleges, or were subject to an informal quota system (especially in the Ivy League), though most of the private schools never officially acknowledged that they had such a policy. As a result, with the return to a peacetime economy in the late 1940s, Baruch and the other CUNY senior colleges admitted a disproportionately large number of Jewish undergraduates, many of whom were intent on pursuing careers in business and accounting.

During the 1960s and 1970s, as much as 70% of the Baruch undergraduate student body was Jewish. These numbers diminished greatly over the ensuing decades, however, as barriers to admission eventually were eliminated at most colleges and universities across the region and the country.[7] Today, Jewish students make up less than 15% of Baruch's undergraduate student body.

In the final year of the period examined in this study (2020), the average combined SAT score for students admitted to Baruch was 1260 and the mean high school GPA was 3.7 (on a 4-point scale).[8] Based on these GPAs and average SAT scores for the college's entering first-year student cohort, which were by far the highest in CUNY, it is clear that Baruch admits a substantial share of the most academically accomplished and capable students in the university.[9] Baruch is today the *only* college in the CUNY system (other than Macaulay Honors College) where the average combined SAT score for admitted students is *above* 1300. This level of academic quality has led to intense competition for admission to its first-year class. While this is a source of justifiable pride for the college, it is also problematic in some respects because it complicates Baruch's effort to meet (or exceed) its admissions diversity goals.

For those fortunate enough to gain admission, and particularly in view of the personal backgrounds and family economic circumstances of many, there is strong motivation to perform well and to graduate quickly. Students understand that doing well at Baruch is likely to lead to a well-paying job or to admission to a high-quality graduate school. In 2020, Baruch's 6-year graduation rate[10] was 72.5% and its first-year retention rate was 87.6%; both were (and remain) the highest in CUNY,[11] and they are among the best for all PHIEs nationwide.

GEOGRAPHIC DISTRIBUTION

The mission of Baruch College and CUNY has always been "to educate the students of the City of New York," and this is clearly reflected in the undergraduate enrollment data. It is actually the case, however, that any student who is a resident of the *state* of New York (whether or not they live within the boundaries of New York City) is eligible to receive in-state tuition rates while attending a CUNY college. Because of Baruch's growing national visibility, including its high 4- and 6-year graduation rates and its top national rankings for social and economic mobility (see below), it now attracts applicants from both New York City and New York State, as well as from other states in the northeast region, and from abroad. On average, more than 15% of each year's admitted class now comes from *outside* of the New York City metropolitan area.

As indicated in Table 2.2, the largest proportion of Baruch's admitted undergraduates from New York City come from the boroughs of Queens and Brooklyn, but a significant percentage come from families who live outside of the city on Long Island or in Westchester County.

Like the rest of CUNY, Baruch is predominantly a commuter school. While the college does maintain a modest number of dormitory rooms at a separate location in Manhattan not far from the campus, most students reside either in their family home or in an apartment (typically, a shared living arrangement). The fact that most students commute to and from Manhattan each day, often from a distance, imposes significant constraints on the academic and student life activities that can be undertaken on the campus, especially after normal class hours.

SOCIAL AND ECONOMIC MOBILITY

One of the main reasons that students apply for admission to Baruch College is due to its reputation for academic quality and rigor combined with its low overall cost, meaning that an individual can expect to graduate with little or no debt and with the likelihood of quickly finding a

Table 2.2. Geographic Distribution of Baruch Undergraduates

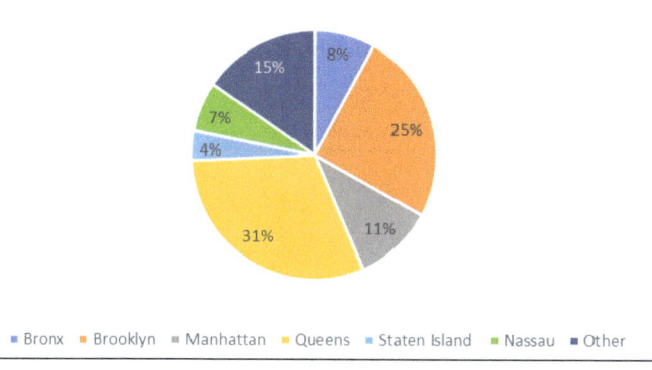

Geographic Distribution

- Bronx: 8%
- Brooklyn: 25%
- Manhattan: 11%
- Queens: 31%
- Staten Island: 4%
- Nassau: 7%
- Other: 15%

Source: Baruch College Fact Sheet, Fall 2020; Also accessible at the following hyperlink: https://nam02.safelinks.protection.outlook.com/?url=https%3A%2F%2Fir.baruch.cuny.edu%2Fwp-content%2Fuploads%2Fsites%2F23%2F2021%2F01%2FFactsheet.Fall_2020_Finalx.pdf&data=05%7C02%7Cmitchel.wallerstein%40baruch.cuny.edu%7C56f811f7e64b40c67cc708dc5bc36e5e%7C6f60f0b35f064e099715989dba8cc7d8%7C0%7C0%7C638486142603820645%7CUnknown%7CTWFpbGZsb3d8eyJWIjoiMC4wLjAwMDAiLCJQIjoiV2luMzIiLCJBTiI6Ik1haWwiLCJXVCI6Mn0%3D%7C0%7C%7C%7C&sdata=Phg4PMwcH5j39UV9%2FKnNYf8jFyFzVRXxQj7EYu6BgSc%3D&reserved=0

well-paying job. It is not unusual for a recent Baruch graduate to be making a higher starting salary in their first job than the rest of their family's *combined* income. When this happy situation occurs, it is obviously life-changing not just for the student but for the entire family, often enabling them to move from the lowest income quintile to a higher standard of living. And because many Baruch students and their families typically live in close-knit ethnic/cultural communities, the socioeconomic elevation of even just a few extended families can also impact the broader community of which they are a part.

For 6 consecutive years during the decade 2010–2020, Baruch College was ranked #1 in the nation in the Social Mobility Index (SMI) developed by CollegeNET.[12] The SMI measures the effectiveness of a particular college or university in moving students from low-income families to well-paying jobs and overall economic success. The SMI is calculated on the basis of five variables: published tuition of the institution, percentage of the school's student body whose family income is below $48,000 (which is slightly below the U.S. median), the 6-year graduation rate, median salary approximately 5 years after graduation, and the institution's endowment. The SMI is calculated using tiers based on three concepts: access, outcome, and institutional capability.[13] Table 2.3 presents the SMI rankings for 15 selected PHEI

Table 2.3. A Comparison of SMI Rankings of 15 PHEI Peer Institutions, 2020

Institution	SMI Rank
CUNY Bernard M. Baruch College	1
California State University, Los Angeles	2
California State University, Fresno	5
California State University, Dominguez Hills	8
CUNY Brooklyn College	9
CUNY Hunter College	12
CUNY Queens College	14
CUNY City College	18
The University of Texas Rio Grande Valley	28
SUNY University at Buffalo	34
SUNY at Albany	35
SUNY Binghamton University	36
University of Illinois Chicago	47
Florida State University	101
University of Maryland, Baltimore County	147

Source: CollegeNET; SocialMobilityIndex.org, 2020

peer institutions with student bodies that present similar demographic and financial characteristics to those of Baruch. These peer institutions will be analyzed further in Chapter 3.

In Baruch's case, the very low CUNY undergraduate tuition, which was $7,462 per year in academic year (AY) 2019–2020, together with the fact that such a high percentage of student families have combined income below $48,000, means that students (or their families) acquire little or no debt because most qualify for New York State's Tuition Assistance Program (TAP) and for federal Pell Grants. As previously noted, three-quarters of Baruch's students graduate in 6 years or less, and because the majority of undergraduates are enrolled in the Zicklin School of Business, they typically go on to well-paying jobs[14] in the private sector.

There is also a second, fairly similar index of student success known as the Economic Mobility Index (EMI), which was developed by the nongovernmental organization Third Way.[15] To assess the degree of economic mobility that institutions of higher education provide, Third Way examined which schools enroll the highest proportion of students from low- and moderate-income backgrounds *and* provide them with a strong return on their educational investment. This index builds upon previous rounds of research focused on generational mobility—most notably, Harvard economist Professor Raj Chetty's intergenerational mobility studies that compare students' post-enrollment incomes to those of their parents.[16] Table 2.4, below, presents the EMI rankings for the same 15 PHEI peer institutions as in Table 2.3 that have student bodies with similar demographic and financial characteristics to those of Baruch. The EMI reveals that Baruch is also in a strong position when it comes to economic advancement based on the relatively modest cost of a Baruch undergraduate degree, as compared with the same group of peer reference institutions.

The first step in creating the EMI was to determine the return on investment that the average low-income student obtains from attending a particular institution of higher education. This was accomplished by using a metric called the Price-to-Earnings Premium (PEP), which is the amount of time it takes for a student to recoup the cost of their education, based on the earnings boost they obtain by attending a given institution. Researchers examined the PEP for very-low-income students, defined as those whose families make $30,000 or less, upon their enrollment in college. They then added into their analyses the number of Pell Grant

Table 2.4. A Comparison of EMI Rankings of 15 PHEI Peer Institutions

Institution	Economic Mobility Index Rank
California State University, Los Angeles	1
California State University, Dominguez Hills	2
The University of Texas Rio Grande Valley	4
California State University, Fresno	7
CUNY City College	11
CUNY Brooklyn College	13
CUNY Bernard M. Baruch College	22
CUNY Hunter College	16
University of Illinois at Chicago	23
CUNY Queens College	24
SUNY at Albany	78
SUNY University at Buffalo	122
Florida State University	131
University of Maryland, Baltimore County	197
SUNY Binghamton University	206

Source: thirdway.org, 2022

students (low- and moderate-income students who receive a federal grant to cover a portion of tuition costs) an institution enrolls to provide a fuller picture of the mobility a school is producing. Finally, to create the EMI, the results of the PEP analysis were applied to the outcomes of low-income students at 1,320 bachelor's degree-granting institutions. Their comparative ranks were then multiplied by the percentage of Pell Grant recipients that each institution enrolls.[17]

ACADEMIC FOCUS

One of the most striking features of the Baruch undergraduate student body is the heavy student preference for the Bachelor of Business Administration (BBA) degree, even though the college today offers a full range of undergraduate majors. In 2020, some 74% of Baruch undergraduates were enrolled in the Zicklin School of Business, while 23% were studying for a degree in the Weissman School of Arts and Sciences and only 3% were pursuing a public policy undergraduate degree in the Marxe School of Public and International Affairs (which is primarily a graduate professional school).

This heavy preference for business is notable in at least two respects. First, of course, it is the direct legacy of Baruch's long history as the premier business school for CUNY, dating back to the time when it was part of City College. Second, it reflects the fact that the (now named and endowed) Zicklin School of Business has achieved a national reputation and ranking as one of leading public business schools in the country. It is, in fact, the largest, fully accredited, public business school in the United States. Finally, it indicates that the academic requirements for admission to the BBA program are fairly rigorous,[18] and as a result the business school tends to attract higher-performing students.

Until fairly recently at least, the reality was that business majors typically were offered higher starting salaries than those graduating with degrees in the liberal arts and sciences or in public affairs. This is probably less true today, however. Indeed, at Baruch students graduating from the Weissman School of Arts and Sciences with degrees in applied mathematics, computer science, and psychology often command high starting salaries as well. This enables them to more quickly pay off any educational debt that they may have accrued during their undergraduate years, which, in turn, gives these students a more favorable debt-to-earnings profile. And it is one of the main reasons why Baruch College has consistently ranked highly on a national basis on measurement standards such as the SMI and the EMI.

The heavy preponderance of business majors at Baruch has a downside as well—namely, it generates near-constant demand for more course sections and more courses. But the problem is that business faculty are among the most highly compensated on a national basis. And the Zicklin School of Business is a highly ranked, research-active public business school with a doctoral program. As a result, the average starting salary in 2022 for a newly recruited *assistant professor* was about $200,000, with a range between $170,000 and $220,000 depending on the field of specialization.[19] By comparison, the average starting salary for a new assistant professor in the Weissman School of Arts and Sciences was in the range of $90,000, and in the Marxe School, most new assistant professors are offered a starting salary just above $100,000. The differential between the three schools becomes even more pronounced at the associate and full professor ranks.

This means that Baruch College must engage in near-constant private fundraising to augment the public "tax levy" salaries paid to its business faculty, to make up the difference between the state-approved and supported contract salary and the *actual* cost of recruiting and/or retaining new faculty or existing faculty who receive outside offers. Perhaps understandably, the significant differential between the average starting salaries in the Zicklin School of Business versus the Weissman School of Arts and Sciences or the Marxe School of Public and International Affairs is occasionally a source of some frustration within the college's faculty ranks.

INTERNATIONAL CHARACTER

Given that New York City has often been described as the "Great Melting Pot," it is perhaps unsurprising that Baruch and CUNY are strongly diverse and international in character. CUNY has been serving the needs of the New York immigrant community for generations. In fact, as noted previously, the express purpose for establishing the Free Academy in 1847 was to educate the swelling numbers of immigrants who were arriving in New York in the late 19th century in order to improve the educational quality of the city's workforce.[20]

Figure 2.1 is a photo of the atrium of the building that houses the Baruch College library and Conference Center, around which 155 flags are displayed, each representing one of the nations of the world that Baruch undergraduates and their families claim as their national origin, though most students are U.S. citizens (or are in the process of obtaining citizenship[21]). Baruch students and their families speak more than 100 different languages in their homes. One has only to look and listen to the students passing by in the corridors of the college's buildings to be struck by their incredible international diversity—there are students from virtually every continent and every ethnicity, race, and national origin.

Figure 2.1. The lobby of Baruch's Library building showing the international flags representing the undergraduate nationalities

During the period from 2010 to 2020, before the onset of the pandemic, Baruch also had a steadily growing *international* student population. In 2018, there were 2,821 international students studying at Baruch.[22] The largest number of international students came primarily from Asia and Africa, and to a lesser extent from South America. The top three sending countries in 2018 were China, South Korea, and India, respectively.[23]

Like the U.S. undergraduates, foreign students come to Baruch primarily to study business. In addition, in recent years the Zicklin School of Business has developed a number of special exchange and joint degree programs with universities in China and in several European countries. One particularly innovative joint program is with the Southwest University for Finance and Economics (SWUFE) in Chengdu, China. There, students are admitted and spend 3 years working toward an undergraduate degree in business at SWUFE, while learning to speak and write English. Then they come to New York for 2 years to pursue a BBA degree in accounting at Baruch—at the end of which they receive degrees from *both* universities. In China, this program is considered highly prestigious, and it is difficult to gain admission.

CAREERS AFTER GRADUATION

Of course, the ultimate attraction for both domestic and foreign students attending Baruch is the possibility of finding a well-paying job at the end of their undergraduate studies. Baruch has, by far, the highest completion rate in the CUNY system, and this can be attributed to students' strong motivation to finish their degree as soon as possible in order to be able to seek and accept a full-time job. Hundreds of companies, most of them based in the New York metropolitan area, recruit on the Baruch campus, and the job fairs are consistently well attended.

I have heard personally from corporate recruiters and people in senior management that they are eager to recruit Baruch graduates. They report that they consistently find them well-prepared and ready to work on day 1. This positive corporate attitude was not the case in earlier decades, when the private sector typically recruited at Baruch and other public colleges and universities primarily for so-called "back of the house" jobs in HR, fulfillment, and so on. The more highly compensated "C-suite track" jobs in finance, marketing, and accounting were often reserved only for graduates of the elite business schools at private colleges and universities. But that situation has now changed rather dramatically. Today, recruiters consider Baruch business graduates to be competitive for *all* types of corporate positions, including those leading to top C-suite appointments.

NATURE VS. NURTURE?

All of the forgoing leads to the question of whether Baruch College is simply the fortunate beneficiary of more talented, better prepared, and (in many cases) more highly motivated students than those applying to CUNY more generally, or whether there is something unique about a Baruch education that propels students forward and enables them to adapt rapidly and effectively to their new educational circumstances. While it is hard to generalize, since each student's situation is unique, the admissions data do support the notion that Baruch is benefiting from a cohort of students who performed well in secondary school and who often have overcome a poor educational environment and other obstacles in the process.

It is also the case, however, that the academic values and competitive atmosphere at Baruch—in all three of its academic schools—*does* put pressure on students to work hard to succeed. As previously noted, the Zicklin School of Business has a specific set of admission requirements that first-year students must fulfill to become candidates for the BBA degree program, which means that those who pass the admission threshold are, by definition, more academically capable and highly motivated. Although many New York City public schools are notoriously weak in preparing students in mathematics, for example, the Zicklin School has long required all entering students to pass introductory calculus in order to qualify for admission to the BBA program.[24] But Baruch also requires that all students complete about half of their curriculum in non-business subject areas, thereby helping them to strengthen and broaden their skill and knowledge base. This is *not* the norm in most undergraduate business programs across the country.

Thus, the ethos of serious commitment to academic achievement seems to permeate the entire undergraduate student body at Baruch, and it is strongly encouraged by the faculty. Indeed, it has been the *modus operandi* of the college since its early days, and it is widely known that enrolling at Baruch requires that a student be prepared to work harder than might be the case at some of the other CUNY colleges. So there is an element of self-selection.[25]

Of course, no student wants to set themselves up to fail, so most simply do not apply for admission to Baruch unless they think they have what it takes and are prepared to work hard. This helps to explain the college's impressively high completion rate. It seems reasonable to conclude on this basis that the subsequent career success of Baruch students beyond the undergraduate degree is likely due to a combination of "nature" *and* "nurture." The college enrolls academically capable students who are more disciplined, more career-focused, and more determined to succeed, and this is supported by Baruch's academic performance data.

CHAPTER 3

How Does Baruch Compare Nationally?

I will not attempt to argue here that Baruch College is unique among U.S. public higher education institutions. Indeed, as I will suggest in this chapter, many of its most notable characteristics are replicated in some form and to some degree in other PHEIs in states across the country. And there are at least two states that subsidize their PHEIs to an even greater extent than does the state of New York.[1] But there are a number of factors that combine to make Baruch notable on both a national and regional basis. Among these are its strong academic quality; affordability; location in midtown Manhattan in New York City; and extraordinary racial, ethnic, and international diversity. As a result, the college has continued to attract many high-performing students from New York City and beyond.

ACADEMIC QUALITY

Academic quality can be measured along a number of dimensions, including (a) the quality, breadth, and rigor of the curriculum; (b) the training, preparedness, reputation, and effectiveness of the faculty; (c) the selectivity of admissions; (d) the academic preparation and quality of the students and their rate of successful degree completion; and (e) the success of students after graduation, whether on the job market or in pursuit of graduate studies. By any of these criteria, Baruch demonstrates a surprisingly and consistently high standard of academic quality.

Curriculum: After the adoption of the CUNY "Pathways initiative"[2] in 2013, the undergraduate general education curriculum at the university became much more standardized. While this had certain benefits, particularly for students seeking to transfer from either one of the CUNY system's 2-year community colleges or from schools outside of CUNY, it has been a dual-edged sword, especially for a school like Baruch. Historically, the college has accepted about three-quarters of its incoming class each year via transfer, but that profile has changed since the start of the pandemic.[3] The college also had, for many years, maintained its own curricular requirements, including the Great Works of Literature program (described in Chapter 1) in the Weissman School of Arts and Sciences, which augmented CUNY degree requirements. The Zicklin School of Business also maintains a series of academic requirements for students seeking admission to the BBA degree program.

It is regrettable that CUNY's effort to standardize curriculum, even though pursued for worthy reasons, has greatly diminished the possibility for curricular flexibility or experimentation on the part of the colleges in the system. In Baruch's case, in particular, the implementation of Pathways clearly had some negative impacts. Many argue, for example, that the elimination of the calculus requirement for admission to the Zicklin School BBA degree program has resulted in reduced quantitative rigor among the enrolled students. Also, by limiting the number of courses outside the major that could be required for completing the major, Baruch was forced to give up the important requirement that all Zicklin School majors had to complete a communication-intensive, liberal arts–focused, upper-division minor. This has diminished the overall value of a Zicklin major and reduced upper-division enrollment in a number of liberal arts departments. The requirement for the minor also produced graduates who were more proficient communicators because they had advanced knowledge in at least one liberal arts field.[4]

On the other hand, the Pathways initiative has made it easier for transfer students to get full academic credit for coursework they previously completed at another institution. And the overall rigor and quality of Baruch's curriculum has continued to be endorsed by the Middle States Association of Colleges and Schools in its decennial reaccreditation reviews.

Faculty Quality: Baruch's faculty is world-class and highly international in character. This latter point is probably unsurprising, given the college's location in the heart of one of the most international cities in the world. Baruch faculty hold doctoral degrees from some of the most prestigious universities in the United States and abroad. There is also a plentiful supply of doctoral talent available in the New York metropolitan area, and there are many promising young academics who are eager to move to New York City.

Nevertheless, faculty recruitment is an increasing challenge for the college for at least two reasons. The first is the high cost of living in New York, which is off-putting to many candidates, especially those who are raising a family. Unless they have a working spouse or partner, it is difficult for many faculty to find affordable housing—and living in Manhattan may be entirely out of the question for most junior faculty due to the cost of rental apartments. This means that many new hires wind up living outside of the city, and they must cope with a long and expensive commute. The second reason is that CUNY salaries are negotiated centrally under a master contract between the university and the Professional Staff Congress (PSC)[5] and must then be approved by the New York state government. While the salary ranges are reasonably competitive with other public universities[6] across the country, they are increasingly out of line with salaries offered at many private colleges and universities, especially for senior faculty.

Baruch also has a special salary challenge that is not shared with most of the other colleges in the CUNY system. It operates the university's flagship business school, the Zicklin School of Business, which offers the MBA degree and also a PhD in business. Faculty salaries in the business school, even at the assistant professor level, may be anywhere from 50% to 100% *higher* than the public pay scale negotiated between CUNY and the PSC and approved by the state.[7] But CUNY does not permit Baruch to pay these premium salaries, above the state-approved contract scale, from public "tax levy" funds. Thus, the additional resources required to recruit—and retain—high-priced business faculty must be raised privately and paid to these individuals as a separate emolument. Moreover, each year the starting salaries in the business school continue to *increase*, seemingly without limit.

Admissions Selectivity: Baruch has for many years consistently been the most selective CUNY college (other than Macaulay Honors College). In 2020, the college received 24,256 applications for first-year admission, and of these, it accepted 9,843 applicants and enrolled 2,243 first-year students, giving it an acceptance rate of 40.5%.[8] This placed Baruch among a relatively small group of public colleges and universities in the "Moderately Selective" admissions category.[9]

Student Academic Quality and Degree Completion: For the incoming class of 2020, the mean combined SAT score was for the first time above 1300 (with a range of 1170–1330).[10] This was 49 points higher than the next-highest-achieving CUNY school, Hunter College.[11] Since 2012, Baruch has been the only school in the CUNY system (again, other than Macaulay Honors College) whose mean SAT score has been consistently above 1200. Also in 2020, the GPA for the incoming first-year class was 3.3 (on a 4-point scale), which also was by far the highest in CUNY. These testing[12] and grade data demonstrate that Baruch continues to attract higher-performing students from the New York City public schools and beyond.

But perhaps even more encouraging than the academic quality of the students applying for admission to Baruch are the data on the rate at which students *complete* their degrees. In 2019, the Baruch 6-year completion rate was 70% and its 4-year completion rate was 44%.[13] (And in the intervening years, the 6-year completion rate has risen still further—to 74%.) It is also interesting to note that the completion rates for students who transfer to Baruch, typically at the start of their third year, are as high as for those who entered as first-year students.[14] While these numbers may appear modest in comparison with the completion rates at many elite private universities, they are considered very strong for students enrolled in a PHEI like Baruch, where the majority of students may not be able to take a full course load each semester because of work and/or family-related obligations. They also compare very favorably with the completion rates at many of the top state universities.

Most Baruch students work, either part- or full-time, while attending college to pay the cost of their education not covered by financial aid and to help support their families. Thus, in many cases, their financial "margin of error" is extremely thin and fragile. So, if they or a member of their immediate family has a major unexpected expense or financial setback, like the loss of a job or an accident or a major illness, they may have no choice other than to withdraw from school (or reduce the number of courses taken) for a semester or even longer. For this reason, it is not uncommon for students, even the highest-performing, to take more than eight academic semesters (4 years) to complete all of their degree requirements.

There is significant variation in terms of 4- and 6-year completion rates among the five CUNY senior colleges, as indicated in Table 3.1. And the same can be said for the completion rates at SUNY and at other similar PHEIs across the country, where there is wide variation as well.

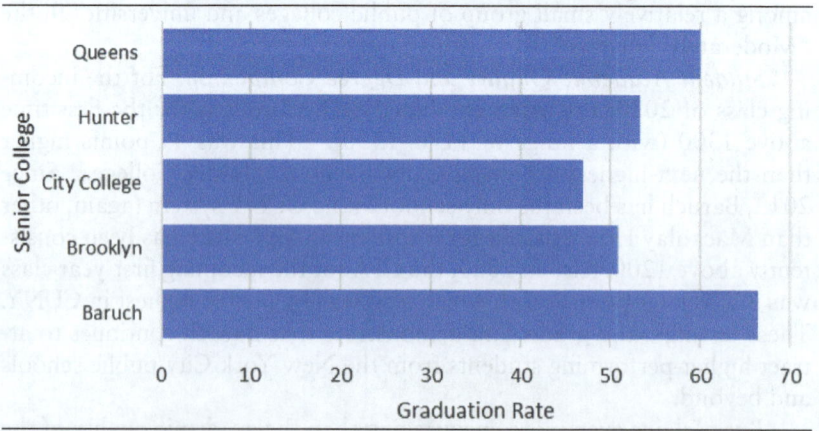

Table 3.1. Six-Year Completion Rates at the CUNY Senior Colleges, 2016

Senior College	Graduation Rate
Queens	60
Hunter	53
City College	47
Brooklyn	51
Baruch	67

Source: CUNY Student Data Book; https://urldefense.proofpoint.com/v2/url?u
=https-3A__public.tableau.com_app_profile_oira.cuny_viz_StudentDataBook
_Enrollment&d=DwMFaQ&c=dTXc8cCP8suVpClwB1HRHQACHN4UFMgL7M
tSjCbKyts&r=9HV09kXmkMupgx68eA27AZukpBvjzNF-5Sc4--NbNAzQ67QdT
a0gMYKawacjxYHj&m=lW0g5lJuXY5B-fhaE67Bt2x84WvHR2jakyCir0XKyL
kVUDJ8Th_UtGrWuLsliaIp&s=Nvae6WFnWLWFu88itq96xwT_GLpJbk7v-62Z
-zBdhdw&e=

Baruch is fortunate to be one of the top-performing public colleges in the nation in terms of degree completion. (Some of the reasons for this success are discussed in Chapter 5.)

Student Success After Graduation: Another measure of the academic quality of any college or university is the rate and nature of student success after graduation. This includes both the percentage of those who have found full-time employment—and the type and quality of their positions—and the percentage who have been accepted to pursue graduate studies. Both are an indication that the value of the education received is recognized by employers and by graduate schools. In Baruch's case, in a 2018 post-graduation survey, 82% of the graduating class[15] had found a job and/or had been accepted to attend graduate school by the fall following the completion of their degree.[16] These are strong numbers by any measure. But Baruch also benefits from the fact that the majority of its undergraduates are studying for the BBA degree. So, there is a ready job market waiting for them right in the New York metropolitan area.

AFFORDABILITY

The overall affordability of higher education has become a paramount concern in recent years, spurred on by data provided in various national rankings.[17] For many students and their families, affordability and the level of debt that would have to be taken on for a student to enroll and successfully graduate is now often a major determining factor in the college selection process. As I have commented elsewhere, college indebtedness upon graduation has now reached such extreme levels that, for many students, it is as if they graduate with "the equivalent of a home mortgage but no house"!

As an academic element of The City University of New York, Baruch's annual tuition, both in-state and out-of-state,[18] is set by the CUNY Board of Trustees, and it is essentially identical across all of the CUNY 4-year colleges, though fees, books, and certain other expenses may vary from one college to another. In academic year 2019–2020, the CUNY undergraduate tuition was $7,462 per year, and the total cost of attending Baruch College was approximately $10,064, making it one of the least expensive PHEIs in the entire country (see Tables 3.2a and 3.2b later in this chapter). In fact, it is still possible to attend Baruch without incurring *any* debt, meaning that those students who qualify for New York state's Tuition Assistance Program, the Excelsior Scholarship program, and the federal Pell Grant program may not be responsible for paying tuition as long as they stay on track to graduate.

In the previous chapter, I focused on Baruch's leading national position in both the Social Mobility and Economic Mobility Indexes. Though the formulas used in each calculation are somewhat different, they both focus on the benefit of low tuition and low indebtedness, combined with relatively high remuneration after graduation, which enables any residual debt to be paid off relatively quickly—in other words, high affordability. This affordability factor should not be underestimated in the college selection decision. As a result, students (and their parents) have increasingly recognized that they can obtain a quality education at Baruch without having to go deeply into debt.

THE GEOGRAPHIC FACTOR

Baruch is fortunate to be located in the heart of lower midtown Manhattan, just north of the well-known (but private) Gramercy Park.[19] As such, I always like to point out that the college enjoys the benefit of being 20 blocks south of the United Nations and about 20 blocks north of Wall Street. Baruch is easily accessible by public transportation, and its students can take advantage of all the cultural, educational, and professional opportunities that New York City has to offer. In addition, given the fact that New York is the business, media, and arts capital of the country, the college's location is a powerful attraction for students, both lifelong residents of the city and state and those from other parts of the United States or from other countries around the world. Students who want to complete their degrees and move directly into the for-profit or nonprofit sectors or work in government or international nongovernmental organizations can readily do so. Typically, most Baruch students have either part- or full-time jobs, or internships, with potential employers during their undergraduate years, and these frequently lead to full-time employment upon graduation.

AN ANALYSIS OF PHEIs COMPARABLE TO BARUCH

As I suggested at the beginning of this chapter, it would be incorrect to argue that Baruch College is unique among public higher education institutions across the United States. But I would contend that the college benefits significantly from a particular combination of academic, financial, geographic, diversity, and other factors that work to its advantage both regionally and nationally.

Tables 3.2a and 3.2b examine 15 comparable PHEIs from six different states across the country. Each institution was selected because its academic, financial, and student profile is similar to that of Baruch, although there are also significant differences among the schools. Perhaps not surprisingly, the four other CUNY senior colleges (Brooklyn, CCNY,

Table 3.2a. Public Institutions of Higher Education Comparable to Baruch

School Name	Location	Undergraduate Population (2019–2020)[1]	Tuition (Annual 2017–2021)[2]	Acceptance Rate (Fall 2020)[3]	Retention Rate	Graduation Rate[4] (6-yr)	Endowment (in Millions of $)
CUNY–Baruch College	New York, NY	15,774	$7,462	41%	88%	73%	222.8
CUNY–Brooklyn College	Brooklyn, NY	14,969	$7,440	50%	82%	58%	98
CUNY–City College of New York	New York, NY	12,587	$7,340	51%	80%	55%	320
CUNY–Hunter College	New York, NY	14,057	$7,382	40%	84%	56%	
CUNY–Queens College	Queens, NY	16,702	$7,538	53%	83%	55%	72
SUNY–University at Albany	Albany, NY	13,182	$10,176	57%	83%	64%	74
SUNY Binghamton University	Vestal, NY	14,333	$10,201	43%	92%	81%	117
SUNY University at Buffalo	Buffalo, NY	20,761	$8,472	67%	65%	40%	53
California State University, Dominguez Hills	Carson, CA	15,873	$6,941	81%	78%	45%	13
California State University, Fresno	Fresno, CA	22,704	$6,643	90%	87%	54%	159
California State University, Los Angeles	Los Angeles, CA	22,832	$6,768	76%	83%	48%	46
Florida State University	Tallahassee, FL	32,543	$5,656	32%	95%	83%	704
University of Illinois Chicago	Chicago, IL	21921	$14,126	73%	82%	59%	2.4 Billion
University of Maryland, Baltimore	Baltimore, MD	10,932	$9,420	70%	87%	70%	102
University of Texas Rio Grande Valley	Edinburg, TX	26,762	$7,813	81%	76%	41%	64

Sources:
[1,2,3,4,5] National Center for Education Statistics, Integrated Post Secondary Data System (IPEDS)
[6] Endowments obtained from each school's website

Table 3.2b. Public Institutions of Higher Education Comparable to Baruch

School Name	Percentage Receiving Undergraduate Financial Aid (AY 2019–2020)[1]	Average Aid Amount[2] (IPEDS)	Percentage Receiving Pell Grants (2019–2020)[3]	Average Debt	Economic Mobility Index	Social Mobility Index Ranking	Price-to-Earnings Premium
CUNY–Baruch College	91%	$9,450	61%	$11,500	22	1	7
CUNY–Brooklyn College	91%	$9,497	66%	$11,819	13	9	17
CUNY–City College of New York	95%	$9,721	70%	$12,500	11	18	24
CUNY–Hunter College	93%	$9,347	61%	$12,500	16	12	13
CUNY–Queens College	90%	$8,737	58%	$12,000	24	14	20
SUNY–University at Albany	76%	$10,149	42%	$19,537	78	35	258
SUNY–Binghamton University	60%	$9,881	25%	$19,500	206	36	133
SUNY–University at Buffalo	89%	$9,597	68%	$21,015	122	34	120
California State University, Dominguez Hills	92%	$10,286	75%	$14,500	2	8	32
California State University, Fresno	84%	$10,745	62%	$15,000	7	5	80
California State University, Los Angeles	94%	$11,315	78%	$13,381	1	2	27
Florida State University	95%	$9,985	25%	$19,973	131	101	53
University of Illinois Chicago	79%	$13,236	57%	$17,400	23	47	130
University of Maryland, Baltimore	65%	$9,379	28%	$21,000	197	147	150
University of Texas Rio Grande Valley	88%	$9,277	71%	$11,661	4	28	69

Sources:
[1,2,3,4,5] National Center for Education Statistics, Integrated Post Secondary Data System (IPEDS)
[6] Endowments obtained from each school's website

Hunter, and Queens) are included, along with three SUNY schools (Albany, Binghamton, and Buffalo) and three California State University schools (Dominguez Hills, Fresno, and Los Angeles). Also included in the analysis are Florida State University; The University of Texas Rio Grande Valley; University of Maryland, Baltimore; and the University of Illinois Chicago. These institutions were each selected based on the following criteria:

Size of the undergraduate student body
Number of first-time college attenders
Annual tuition
Acceptance rate (percentage)
Retention rate (percentage)
Graduation rate (percentage)
Percentage of undergraduates receiving financial aid and average aid amount
Percentage of undergraduates receiving Pell Grants
Average student debt upon graduation
Social Mobility and Economic Mobility Index rankings
Price-to-earnings premium (i.e., the number of years required to pay down total college debt)
Number of residential students vs. commuters
Presence on campus of a business or engineering school

These specific criteria were chosen because they make it possible to compare a group of disparate PHEIs across six states. All of the schools included are from states with large and successful public higher education systems. All of the schools also display the advantages of publicly funded colleges and universities—low tuition rates, high availability of financial aid, low debt upon graduation, and reasonably selective admissions with strong measures of academic success in terms of retention and graduation rates. Finally, the graduates of these institutions demonstrate relatively high social and economic mobility after receiving their undergraduate degrees. This means that students significantly improve their socioeconomic status, due to a strong "price-earnings premium" that enables them to quickly pay down and eliminate any remaining higher education debt while reaping the financial benefits of having received a college degree.

Other comparative factors analyzed (but not shown in the table) included whether each institution was predominantly a residential or a commuter school and whether each had business or engineering degree programs available to undergraduates. The former affects the overall cost of obtaining a degree—that is, if a student must pay for room and board, in addition to tuition, books, etc., rather than living at home. The latter factor is included based on the strong indication that students graduating with undergraduate degrees in more highly compensated professions, like business or engineering, can more quickly improve their financial situation. In addition, their higher level of compensation over the course of a career also makes it possible for them to "give back" to their alma mater in the form of annual donations and, later, significant endowment gifts.

The data presented in the tables suggest that Baruch benefits from the "Goldilocks effect" in relation to the other 14 schools studied. Its tuition is not the lowest; its admissions selectivity, retention, and graduation rates are not the highest, nor is the percentage of those receiving financial aid. But it performs very well in comparison to the other 14 peer institutions across *all* of these categories, and it is a national leader in some—for example, economic and social mobility. When all of these factors are taken into account, Baruch emerges from this cohort of selected peer institutions as one of the leading PHEIs in the country.

CHAPTER 4

Challenges Facing Baruch and Other Public Higher Education Institutions

It must be said that the current public perception of public higher education institutions is somewhat mixed. On the one hand, these colleges and universities are recognized and valued for offering a less expensive alternative to the increasingly unaffordable total cost[1] of many private higher education institutions. In 2020, the average tuition cost for all private colleges and universities was $35,852 per year, as compared to $9,375 per year for PHEIs.[2] The average annual tuition cost for that same year at the "Ivy League-Plus" schools (which includes the Ivy League schools and similar elite institutions such as Stanford, the University of Chicago, and Duke) exceeded $60,000. Today, the *total* cost at many of these elite schools is approaching $90,000 per year,[3] and a few may soon break through the $100,000 per year barrier.[4] Clearly, in the absence of deep discounts and other forms of financial aid, a price tag of this magnitude is simply beyond the means of most middle-class families, even if they are willing to assume a heavy debt burden, and it is entirely out of reach for families at the lower end of the economic spectrum.

On the other hand, parents and students worry that, faced with flat or declining state support, generally modest private endowment resources,[5] inadequate and often obsolete facilities, significantly larger class sizes, and less well paid faculty, many PHEIs may not be capable of offering a first-class undergraduate education. Unquestionably, there are many challenges on public campuses, and the resources required to address them are often lacking. Yet, for many families, especially those with limited economic resources, there may be no other option, unless their student is academically gifted or is recruited as a Division I or II athlete and qualifies for an athletic scholarship.

POLITICAL SUPPORT FOR PUBLIC HIGHER EDUCATION

Given that most PHEIs derive the largest share of their operating budgets from the state in which they are located, sustaining political support in state legislatures and in governors' offices is essential. This is certainly the case for CUNY and its affiliated colleges. Higher education in general—and CUNY in particular—has not always fared well in the rough and tumble give-and-take politics of the annual budget process. While CUNY does have a loyal and supportive contingent of elected representatives from the New York City metropolitan area, they are often outvoted (and/or outmaneuvered) by the larger cohort of legislators representing other parts of the state, who want to keep the academic jobs and students in their home districts. As a result, in CUNY's case, legislators representing New York City must constantly push back against perceived "upstate bias," and the view in Albany that CUNY doesn't really need additional resources from the state, given its location in wealthy New York City.

New York is one of only a limited number of states that has *two* large and separate, publicly supported university systems—in this case, one located in New York City and the other widely dispersed throughout the rest of the state. The two systems consult and coordinate only infrequently on matters related to the state budget. In fact, they generally perceive the budget process as a zero-sum game; and in a real sense, they are in direct competition with each other for a limited pot of state higher education resources.

In recent years at least, CUNY has had an additional problem: It was not a high priority—or, at times, a priority at all—for some governors. Governor Andrew Cuomo, for example, did not like the fact that he did not have complete control of the CUNY Board of Trustees,[6] and he tended to take the mostly Democratic voters of New York City for granted. Indeed, Cuomo seemed far more interested in courting political support from upstate communities where the SUNY campuses were located. Thus, as may be observed in Table 4.1, state support for CUNY did not keep pace with the increases granted to the SUNY system during the period from 2010 to 2020. While it is possible that this apparent anti-CUNY bias may diminish under the leadership of a different governor, it is difficult to avoid the conclusion that there is little motivation in Albany to change the current allocation of state budget resources for higher education.

Similar struggles for political influence over the allocation of limited state higher education resources exist in other states as well, including some of the PHEIs identified in the previous chapter in Tables 3.2a and 3.2b. In the state of California, for example, there is a longstanding competition for budget resources between the University of California system,[7] the California State system,[8] and the statewide system of 116 community colleges. But the appropriation process in California does not appear to have the same kind of sharp, upstate-downstate division that occurs in New York. Rather, in the California case, it seems to be more a competition between the three separate levels of the state public higher

Figure 4.1. State Support for Public Higher Education, 2010–2020

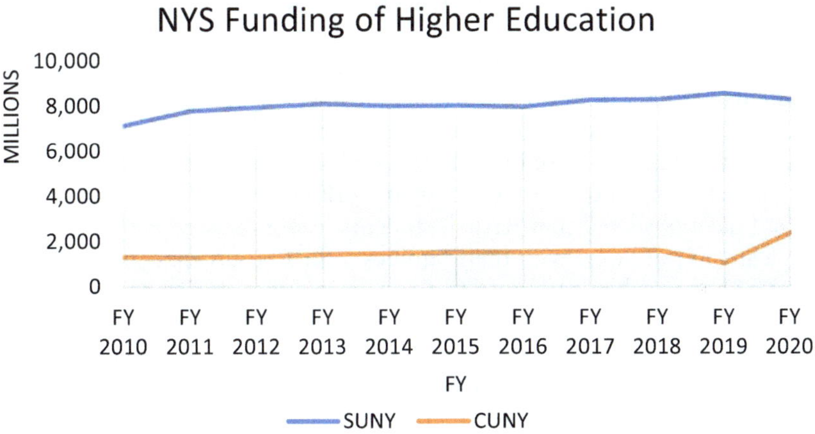

NYS Funding of Higher Education

[Line chart, MILLIONS on y-axis (0 to 10,000), FY 2010 through FY 2020 on x-axis. SUNY line remains around 7,500–8,500 million across the period; CUNY line remains around 1,500 million, dipping in FY 2019 and rising to about 2,000+ in FY 2020.]

— SUNY   — CUNY

Source: 2023–2024 State of New York Open Budget: Budget & Actuals: Higher Education, https://openbudget.ny.gov/overview/overview-spendFunction.html

education system. In Illinois, on the other hand, there has long been an "upstate-downstate" competition in the allocation of resources between the University of Illinois at Urbana-Champaign, the University of Illinois at Chicago, and the University of Illinois at Springfield, despite the fact all three schools operate within the *same* system. These examples beg two other closely related questions: (1) to what extent do campuses located in the same system have any independent leverage over state budget decisions?, and (2) are campuses that are relatively more successful, both academically and financially, inherently disadvantaged in a state that funds *systems* rather than campuses? Virginia, for example, has a state higher education system, but it funds at the campus level, and New Jersey does the same.[9]

The budgetary outcome in most states depends on the extent to which each university can successfully lobby legislators and the governor's office for funds to address specific needs and can mobilize political influence at key junctures when the final budget "put's and take's" are being negotiated, often behind closed doors. In this respect, Baruch and the other colleges of the CUNY system are at a serious disadvantage, given that lobbying and efforts to influence the budget outcome are primarily the responsibility of the university's chancellery.[10] This fact notwithstanding, the other CUNY college presidents and I spent many days each year traveling to Albany and to district offices to meet with key legislators and their staffs to educate them regarding individual college budget priorities and urgent needs for the upcoming fiscal year. It was never clear to me, however, that *any* of these efforts made a significant difference regarding the final budget outcome.[11]

ADDRESSING THE NEEDS OF STUDENTS WHO COMMUTE AND WORK

As a college of more than 20,000 students, virtually all of whom commute daily and work either part- or full-time, the needs, challenges, and opportunities on the campus are very different than at a residential college or university, where most of the students live either on the campus or very close by and where those who work generally do so on the campus. I have observed that Baruch students lead a "triangular life"—they typically live at home with their families or in a group apartment outside of Manhattan; they commute to the college either during the day or in the evening; and they work at a separate location in order to support themselves, pay the cost of their education, and contribute to the family's total income. Their lives are therefore extraordinarily busy, and it is not uncommon for them to wind up doing the assigned course reading while commuting or late at night at home.

This demanding triangular life rhythm creates significant challenges for the college as well. Students tend to be on campus only during specific hours and on specific days, normally around the time that their classes are scheduled to meet,[12] which can make it difficult for them to accomplish their basic administrative needs and requirements, such as arranging appointments with faculty or with the registrar, bursar, and other college offices. It also creates difficult challenges for the Office of Student Life. For example, it makes it very difficult to convince undergraduate students to return to the campus in the evening for important events and activities[13] or to monitor and engage with students who may be having emotional or psychological difficulties.[14]

This latter point is especially important because it is considerably more difficult on a commuter campus to identify and track students who are struggling academically or who may be experiencing psychological problems. The COVID-19 pandemic only exacerbated these challenges while the college was shut down. On a residential campus, the struggling student is "in the community" (they would typically be living in a dormitory room on campus, taking meals at a dining hall, etc.), and thus they would be identified by a dorm resident assistant (RA) or even by fellow students who know their normal patterns and overall situation.

But on a commuter campus, especially one that is located in the heart of a very large city, there is much less proximity and regular contact and, therefore, less individual familiarity. As a result, students can, and sometimes do, fall through the cracks.[15] Often, it is only when a faculty member reports that a student has not been attending class, or is failing a course, that the Baruch Counseling Center is alerted. Like most academic institutions, the college does maintain a Crisis Intervention Team, which is staffed by professionals and prepared to act when a student in crisis is identified. Unfortunately, however, some struggling students remain off the radar, sometimes with tragic results.[16]

DEALING WITH A UNIONIZED FACULTY AND STAFF

It is not uncommon to find a strong union presence on campus in many PHEIs. In most states, virtually all faculty and staff are state employees, since they are paid from tax levy resources. This may, in some cases, limit the extent to which faculty or staff unions are able to strike or resort to other job actions, and in some cases such activities are banned outright. But in states where the role and rights of unions are recognized, their presence offers two important advantages. First, it enables the negotiation of a collective contract that applies to everyone holding the same type of job. And second, it provides a forum for raising issues that are common to all those represented by the union—for example, regarding health benefits, workload requirements, and so on.

We are now in an era where many PHEIs—and even some private institutions—rely increasingly on adjunct faculty to provide a sizable share of the undergraduate teaching duties, due to their lower pay scale, lack of benefits, and the flexibility to discontinue their employment if state support is reduced or if their expertise is no longer needed (since they are, by definition, not on a tenure track). And it is notable that unions have made some headway in recent years in representing the needs of this segment of the academic workforce. At CUNY, for example, the union representing faculty and staff, which is known as the Professional Staff Congress (PSC),[17] was recently able for the first time to negotiate some limited health-care coverage for certain categories of *adjunct* faculty. But progress has been slow and uneven, especially when public budgets for higher education are flat or declining in real terms.

Regular faculty, both those already tenured and those who are on a tenure track, often have a different set of economic and social concerns that they wish to raise with university management than do the adjunct faculty or staff. Since it is often infeasible to raise such matters on an individual basis, the contract renewal process offers an important way of doing so. Perhaps not surprisingly, the biggest issue is almost always the need to increase salaries to keep pace with the cost of living. There is a common perception that, similar to most other public colleges and universities across the country, wages at CUNY have not kept pace with the private institution pay scales.

That said, given the constraints on state resources, it is rarely possible for faculty at PHEIs to "catch up" from a salary standpoint; most often, it is instead a question of whether management can offer sufficient pay increases to keep pace with inflation. Perhaps needless to say, the high rate of inflation that followed the pandemic made this an especially important issue in contract negotiations. In addition, the high cost of living in New York City is a particularly important issue at CUNY, and as earlier noted, many university employees, both faculty and staff, often are forced to live far beyond the boundaries of New York City for this reason. But the cost savings they achieve by living in places with less expensive housing may be partly neutralized by the cost of commuting to Manhattan to teach or work.

Among the other issues of concern to university unions are workload requirements, research support, sabbatical policies, and retirement and other social benefits, such as health care and family and medical leave. In general, I believe that the existence of unions on public campuses has been a net plus for those they represent, enabling greater progress than might have otherwise been possible in their absence.[18] As previously noted, the situation at CUNY is complicated by the fact that a single union, the PSC, represents both faculty and many categories of staff, and the groups often have differing needs and concerns.

Given the size and complexity of CUNY as an institution, and especially in view of the shared state-city responsibility for CUNY's operating budget, it is understandable that those who work at the institution have opted for collective representation. And the PSC has succeeded in gaining increased wages, improved benefits, and better working conditions for faculty and staff alike during its more than 50 years of existence.[19] But this success has also come at a price.

For one thing, the PSC is guided by the principle that all faculty have *equal* value across all disciplines, and it has resisted the idea of differentiated compensation based on market price signals in various disciplines (e.g., business, medicine, or engineering vs. the liberal arts). In Baruch's case, for example, faculty salaries in the Zicklin School of Business run anywhere from 40% to 100% *higher* at all professorial levels (assistant, associate, and full) than in the college's Weissman School of Arts and Sciences. This means that each year Baruch must find the financial resources to recruit *and retain* quality business faculty, who typically are paid well beyond the salary scales negotiated collectively by the PSC and approved by the state. This has required that Baruch annually raise a substantial amount of *private* funds to augment the state-supported salaries, primarily for its business faculty. As business school salaries continue to escalate (and there is no end in sight), this has become a serious challenge for the college's leadership.

The PSC has also been criticized, at times, for excessive political and social activism, and for taking public positions that sometimes do not reflect the views of its broadly diverse membership. While some of its positions appear laudable, others have needlessly stirred up controversy on the campuses. [20] An example of the latter was a PSC resolution adopted in June 2021 "In Support of the Palestinian People," which broadly condemned the state of Israel and called for subsequent consideration by the PSC of possible support for the Boycott, Divestment, and Sanctions (BDS) movement against Israel.[21] The adoption of this resolution created a strong backlash among Jewish faculty and staff at CUNY. In fact, dozens of union members quit the PSC because of the resolution (which they have the right to do, even though they are still represented by the union in collective bargaining), and some questioned why the union was focused on an issue that appeared entirely unrelated to its mission.[22]

At Baruch, such controversies have made the PSC union sometimes appear to be opposed to the interests and personal views of some members of the college's faculty and staff. This is particularly the case in the Zicklin School of Business, where many faculty choose *not* to participate in the PSC and do not find the union to be sympathetic to or interested in addressing their concerns. While collective bargaining remains relevant, particularly for faculty in the liberal arts disciplines, who have tended historically to be undercompensated, some university faculty in disciplines such as business, medicine, law, and engineering do not perceive that the union represents or is supportive of their interests.

DEALING WITH SEVERE SPACE CONSTRAINTS AND AGING FACILITIES

The Baruch College campus today consists of seven buildings located along four blocks of Lexington Avenue in lower midtown Manhattan, just north of Gramercy Park. The campus is divided by the main cross-town thoroughfare of 23rd Street, and some refer to this division (semi-humorously) as the "north campus" and the "south campus." The college's original building is located at the corner of Lexington Avenue and 23rd Street.[23] It opened in 1929 on the site where the Free Academy previously stood (see Chapter 1). For the next 40 years, the building housed the entire college. But after 1968, when Baruch became a fully independent senior college in the CUNY system, the school's student population began to increase rapidly, and soon it could no longer be accommodated in a single building.

As a result, two additional buildings[24] were acquired by CUNY, but the college was soon forced to lease *additional* academic space in nearby office buildings in the area, at an annual cost of $22 million,[25] simply to accommodate the growth. Then, in 1994, under the leadership of then Baruch President Matthew Goldstein, the state agreed to appropriate more than $300 million to build a new primary academic building for the college, which later became known as the Newman Vertical Campus. The building is more than 1 million square feet[26] and consists of 14 floors, encompassing almost an entire city block. It includes 102 classrooms, 14 research labs, 36 computer labs, more than 500 offices, 2 auditoriums, a concert venue, a black box theater, an Olympic-size swimming pool, and 2 basketball gyms.[27] The Newman Vertical Campus opened in 2001 and within a decade it, too, could not fully accommodate the needs of the growing college, which by then had a population of more than 17,000 students.

Today, Baruch faces a threefold facilities challenge. The first is that many of its buildings are old (some close to 100 years), and they are in need of serious renovation and modernization. But given the college's dependence on public "tax levy" funds for such capital projects, progress occurs at a glacial pace. For example, when I arrived in 2010 to take up my duties as president, I was briefed on the details of a plan to completely renovate and reorganize the college's original building at 17 Lexington Avenue. The work was to be undertaken in six phases, and I was assured that Phase 1 would commence within 6 months of my arrival—*3 years later*, I was still waiting to see the first shovel in the ground. As it turned out, it took *an additional* 4 years for the necessary capital funds to be appropriated by the state, for the construction plans to be finalized, for the contracts to be bid out, and for the work to commence. And that was just for the *first* phase of a project! Indeed, at the rate that the work has proceeded, it is possible that the project may not be fully complete until about the time of the college's centenary—in 2068!

The appropriation of funds to renovate Baruch and CUNY buildings always must compete, of course, with other larger and more urgent state priorities. In recent years, these have included (a) the construction of a new bridge across the Hudson River to replace the deteriorated Tappan Zee Bridge, (b) the rebuilding of LaGuardia Airport, (c) the construction of the Moynihan Train Hall and the renovation of Penn Station, and (d) several other large infrastructure projects such as a new train tunnel under the Hudson River. Thus, as seen from the viewpoint of government officials in Albany, Baruch's building renovation project (and other similar projects at CUNY) is barely even on the radar—and if it is, it remains a *very* low priority.

The second challenge concerns the neighborhood in which Baruch College "lives" in lower midtown Manhattan. Real estate prices in the area between Gramercy Park and Madison Square Park are expensive, and prior to the pandemic, they were increasing rapidly. By 2020, the market had already reached a price point where it was essentially impossible for a publicly funded institution like Baruch to raise sufficient public or private funds to purchase an existing building or even to buy the land needed to construct a building in the area. And given the intense competition for real estate in Manhattan, private developers, who typically have deep private financial backing, can usually outbid a not-for-profit organization.

During my tenure as president, we experienced this reality firsthand. One of Baruch's enduring needs for many decades had been for a dedicated residential dormitory space to house students from outside of the New York area or who came from abroad, as well a student center to house student government and other activities. Students who come from outside of New York are obviously in need of low-cost and safe housing during their undergraduate years. In fact, it had long been the case that Baruch was the only school among the five CUNY senior colleges that did not have a dedicated dormitory building located on or very near its campus.

In 2011, an old residential hotel that happened to be located immediately adjacent to the Baruch campus became available for lease or purchase. After consultation with and deliberation by the trustees of the Baruch College Fund, which is the private fundraising foundation connected with the college (discussed in detail later in this chapter), Baruch decided (with CUNY's support) to pursue a long-term ground lease on the building with the intention of turning it into a dormitory and a student center.

Although there were multiple expressions of interest in the hotel property, in the end there were only two serious bidders: Baruch College and a company known for developing boutique hotels in New York and other cities around the country. To no one's surprise—but many people's great regret—the college was ultimately *outbid* by the private developer. Baruch simply could not mobilize sufficient financial resources to match the offers made by the private company. Given the close proximity of this building to the Baruch campus, the inability to obtain the lease was a serious disappointment and setback, and it resulted in a fundamental reassessment of whether the college really had the financial capacity to pursue real estate opportunities in midtown Manhattan.

The third challenge, which is also a direct result of the lack of financial resources to purchase or lease space in pricey midtown Manhattan, is that the amount of Baruch's per capita academic space continues to shrink as total enrollment grows. Baruch's total student population (undergraduate and graduate) increased from about 17,000 students in 2010–2011 to almost 19,000 students in 2019–2020. And today, the college's total student population exceeds 20,000. All of this growth has occurred without *any* parallel increase in available classrooms or other academic space. In fact, the increase in the college's total student population was only possible because a significant number of undergraduate and graduate courses were moved to either a synchronous or an asynchronous online format.

While this change was an expedient and necessary short-term solution to the space problem, driven by the urgency of the unprecedented COVID-19 pandemic, the college's underlying space constraints remain.

According to CUNY's own estimate in 2010, Baruch College was short by at least 100,000 net usable square feet of academic space,[28] and that shortage has only grown due to the college's continuing student population increase. It is simply not possible to shoehorn a growing population of undergraduate and graduate students into a static number of classrooms and seats—and shifting even more classes online is not a satisfactory solution either. Therefore, unless and until CUNY and the state of New York can identify the necessary resources to enable Baruch to lease or buy another academic building, the college will likely be forced to cap its enrollment.

One additional space-related challenge for Baruch is worth focusing on here—namely, the lack of *outdoor* space. This is a problem that successive Baruch presidents have been aware of for many decades. Baruch is the quintessential *urban* institution. It is surrounded on all sides by pavement and building density, and there is no open outdoor space. The college itself consists entirely of medium-rise buildings, the tallest of which is 17 stories.[29] Indeed, I discovered upon my arrival that there was effectively *no* outdoor campus and, therefore, no place for students, faculty, and staff to meet or to recreate.[30] At one point I challenged a group of students to find a single patch of grass or greenery (other than the city-planted trees along the sidewalks) in the vicinity of the college, but they were unable to do so. Beyond the fact that Baruch's physical configuration was not aesthetically appealing or environmentally friendly, the lack of any outdoor common space meant that it was impossible to hold outdoor events, to enable people to interact or simply sit and eat lunch in the good weather. The lack of outdoor space has always been a serious constraint in terms of the objective of improving college-wide morale and esprit de corps.

Thus, in 2011, during my first year as president, we decided to launch a campaign to dramatically change this situation. We saw an opportunity to take advantage of the city's "Plaza Program," which had been initiated by then New York Mayor Michael Bloomberg to establish new outdoor *pedestrian* spaces in all five boroughs of the city by closing parts of city streets and restricting them for pedestrian uses only. Among the most notable examples of the program's success are the plazas that were constructed in Times Square and in Herald Square near the Macy's flagship department store along Broadway. But similar pedestrian spaces have also been built in other locations around the city.

We launched the campaign by enlisting the support of Baruch's Student Government Association and then seeking the support and approval of the local community board, and both were quickly forthcoming. It did not take too much convincing in either case, given that Baruch had *zero* outdoor space and it was an established fact the Gramercy and Flatiron neighborhoods in Manhattan had the *least* amount of outdoor public space per capita in the entire city.[31] But the entire effort hinged on gaining the city's agreement to permanently close one block of East 25th Street, between Third and Lexington Avenues, and to share in the cost of constructing the plaza. Our argument was strengthened, in this regard, by the fact that 25th Street dead-ends at Madison Square Park, so it was not a cross-town thoroughfare.

As it turned out, the Baruch Plaza, which later came to be known officially as Clivner=Field Plaza, named after its two largest alumni benefactors, was one of the last plaza projects approved by the outgoing Bloomberg administration. While gaining city approval in principle for the project was a critical first step, it turned out to be only the *beginning* of the process. There followed multiple *years* spent navigating through the maze of New York City government agencies, including the departments of Planning, Public Works, Design and Construction, as well as NYPD and FDNY, and meeting all of the requirements and regulations that each imposed. Then the project had to be publicly bid out, because it was to be undertaken as a public-private partnership between the city and Baruch College.[32] Finally, the college had to undertake a major private fundraising campaign to meet its commitment to match the city's contribution.[33] And then the pandemic happened, which slowed construction progress to an absolutely glacial pace.

The combination of all these factors meant that a project that was conceived and initiated in 2011 required fully 10 years to complete! Construction was finished in the spring of 2021, and Clivner=Field Plaza was formally dedicated the following October. But it was, however, well worth the wait.[34] After many decades, Baruch students, faculty, and staff *finally* had a safe and attractive outdoor space in which to gather, despite the fact that the college is located in the heart of busy and traffic-clogged midtown Manhattan. Moreover, the surrounding community was able to take full advantage of the new public space for its own gatherings and events. It has been a game-changer for the college, and it adds significantly to the school's appeal to prospective students.

MOBILIZING PRIVATE PHILANTHROPIC SUPPORT FOR A PUBLIC INSTITUTION

As noted above, the Baruch Plaza project would not have been possible without the strong philanthropic support provided by the Baruch College community—alumni, current students, faculty, staff, and friends in the local community. The ability to mobilize significant private giving, not just for a major project like the plaza but also the annual support that helps to advance the college more generally, has been a hallmark of the school for decades. Clearly, many Baruch alumni have recognized that those who preceded them at the college contributed generously through

Figure 4.2. A Photo of the Completed Clivner=Field Plaza at Baruch College

the Baruch College Fund, which helped to raise the school's academic quality and visibility, and in the process helped to make *their* degrees more valuable and prestigious. These alumni understand that they benefited from the generosity of others during their undergraduate years, and they have adopted a "pay it forward" philosophy, understanding that they had an obligation to do the same, when their financial situation permitted, to help the next generation of students.

Such a "pay it forward" attitude is not all that common, especially at *publicly* funded institutions like Baruch. Indeed, during my tenure, I would occasionally encounter skeptical alumni, who would state some version of the following: "Why should I contribute my private funds to a *public* institution that receives direct support from the state of New York? Isn't that what my tax dollars are for?" The response I would give them is that, while it is obviously correct that Baruch does receive an annual tax levy budget allocation, these funds account for only 27.4% of the college's total annual operating budget. Tuition paid by students and their families accounts for another 57.7%, and the remaining 14.9% must come from private philanthropy and other sources.[35] So, private support for a public institution, which does not come with the same restrictions on use as state tax levy dollars, is absolutely essential; and it has enabled Baruch to establish and maintain a higher level of quality and programs than would otherwise be possible.

All institutions of higher education, both public and private, actively seek the support of their alumni, as well as philanthropic contributions from private foundations, corporations, and so forth in order to balance their budgets and to start new initiatives. But the national data demonstrate that *private* colleges and universities enjoy substantially higher rates of alumni giving than do PHEIs.[36] Thus, while the rate of private giving to Baruch is still well below the average rate of giving to most of the leading private colleges and universities, it has been sufficiently robust to enable the college to offer a variety of services, programs, and financial support that many other PHEIs (including many of the other senior colleges within CUNY) simply cannot provide. It has, for example, enabled Baruch to (a) establish special programs and academic support services, (b) subsidize the salaries of some of its most outstanding faculty to help recruit and retain them, and (c) provide student scholarships and other financial assistance. Most of this giving flows to the college through the Baruch College Fund (BCF), the college's private fundraising foundation, which was established in February 1969, just a year after Baruch became an independent senior college within the CUNY system.

Another advantage that Baruch has had, until recent years, is that a large percentage of its alumni were Jewish. I want to be clear, in this regard, that I am not intending to make a statement of religious preference or bias. Rather, this is meant to underscore the fact that the Jewish religion has a moral and social tradition known as *"tzedakah,"* which means the duty to make charitable gifts to help those less fortunate. As noted in Chapter 1, Jewish students enrolled in CUNY—and particularly at City College and later Baruch College—in large numbers during the 20th century, in part because they were being denied admission to private higher education institutions, including the Ivy League schools, due to anti-Semitic admission policies. As a result, Jews were for many years *over*represented in the CUNY student body—and this demographic trend naturally continued once these student cohorts became alumni. As recently as the 1960s and early 1970s, for example, approximately 70% of the Baruch undergraduate population was Jewish.

The combination of two factors unique to Baruch—namely, the large number of alumni who had achieved great financial success in the business world, and the large proportion of these same alumni who were Jewish and therefore motivated to give back charitably to the college—contributed to a philanthropic financial windfall. The result is that Baruch is today the *only* college within the CUNY system to have *all* of its major academic units (schools) named and endowed—and the generous alumni donors who endowed all three schools[37] happen to be of

Jewish background. In addition, the largest *overall* donor to the college, the late William Newman, whose generous philanthropy helped to provide Baruch with an award-winning library, the Newman Vertical Campus, and a number of other important facilities and programs, was as well.

For this same reason, the BCF was able to establish a tradition of holding an annual, well-attended and financially successful gala fundraising dinner. In most years, the Bernard Baruch Dinner has raised more than a million dollars for the benefit of the college's Annual Fund, and it has now been held for 35 years. It has been a major contributor to the private support raised by the college, as well as a social highlight for the alumni and friends of the college who attend.

As previously noted, the ethnic makeup of Baruch College has changed dramatically over recent decades, and the Jewish student population has now declined significantly. Today, the Jewish population at Baruch represents less than 15% of the undergraduate student body. As a result, the number of Jewish alumni is also now declining as well. This will present a serious fundraising challenge for future leaders of the college and for its fundraising foundation, the BCF. Baruch will have to find ways to identify and successfully engage a new cohort of wealthy alumni donors from among the *other* ethnic and racial groups who today represent the majority of the college's student body.

CHAPTER 5

Indicators of Baruch's Success

Given the variety of challenges enumerated in the preceding chapters, it is useful to assess how Baruch has responded—that is, to identify the areas in which it has achieved noteworthy success. As I suggested in the introduction to this volume, Baruch's many achievements have made it a "positive outlier" within a university system that has been and remains chronically underresourced, and which has, as a result, underachieved in many respects. Despite the financial and programmatic constraints imposed by its status as a state-supported institution, Baruch has found ways of coping within an often difficult and obstacle-laden political, economic, and academic environment, and it has managed to succeed where many of its institutional peers have struggled.

What makes this idea somewhat surprising and unexpected is that Baruch College is only one college within the enormous CUNY system that consists of 25 separate campuses. As such, Baruch lacks the authority to create its own independent budget, to negotiate its own labor contracts, or even to teach a customized undergraduate curriculum. And this obviously begs the question: How has it avoided being forced to the "lowest common denominator," along with the other CUNY colleges? In some respects, it has *not* been able to avoid this fate, since it is not an independent legal entity—i.e., all of the CUNY colleges and graduate schools exist under the legal imprimatur of The City University of New York and under the policy control of its board of trustees. But Baruch has in many cases been able to identify workarounds and other creative solutions that typically involve the use of private funds, which have helped it avoid some of the most debilitating or restrictive aspects that come with being a part of a large, publicly funded university.

During my tenure as president, I commented occasionally to colleagues that CUNY's main problem was that "it can't get out of its own way." I meant by this that the university too often is held back by outdated rules and procedures, many of which appear to exist only as institutional "folklore"—meaning that it was not evident that they were the result of specific state or city laws or regulations. This rule-bound inflexibility and inability to act often stifles academic and administrative creativity and innovation, and it prevents modernization and change in a variety of ways.

Admittedly, a large part of CUNY's risk aversion and bureaucratic sclerosis was and is the inevitable result of the resentful (and sometimes openly hostile) attitude of the state government in Albany, where some felt that funding CUNY was a burden that should once again become the responsibility of New York City.[1] There was always a fear in the CUNY chancellery (which was sometimes realized) that the state might cut or flatline the budget, especially if CUNY did not appear to "toe the line," or if it made excessive financial demands. There was also a perception that the State University of New York (SUNY) consistently seemed to fare better in the annual budget process, due in large part to the fact that (a) it is headquartered in Albany only a stone's throw from the governor's office and the state legislature, and (b) it has effectively mobilized upstate political interests to put pressure the governor's office.

Yet another reason for CUNY's lack of innovation and forward momentum, according to some, is the makeup of its board of trustees. Due to the power-sharing formula worked out in the wake of the city's financial crisis, two-thirds of the CUNY board of trustees are appointed by the governor and one-third is appointed by the New York City mayor. And there are no requirements that board nominees of either political leader have relevant experience or expertise in academic administration or higher education. As a result, with some notable exceptions, trustee appointees have too often lacked appropriate expertise, and such board appointments have been used either as a reward for political support or as a way to insert loyalists on the CUNY board to keep an eye on things and to assure the sitting governor that decisions are taken only with her/his approval. As a result, the CUNY board of trustees has only rarely demonstrated a willingness to act as public advocates for CUNY's urgent financial needs with the state or city governments.

Despite these institutional and political limitations, Baruch College managed to prosper and grow over the past few decades. It clearly benefited from the perception that it is the most academically competitive college in the CUNY system (other than Macaulay Honors College) and that earning an undergraduate Baruch degree is the gateway to a good job or to prestigious graduate school admission. Of course, it also helps that Baruch operates CUNY's flagship business school, the Zicklin School of Business. Frequently, families have been eager for their sons and daughters to gain admission to the Zicklin School, believing (rightly) that a Zicklin degree is the ticket to a better life not only for their child but also for the entire family.

Indicators of Baruch's Success

INCREASING QUALITY OF THE STUDENT BODY

When I arrived at Baruch in 2010, the mean combined SAT score for first-year students was hovering just below 1200, which, while the highest in CUNY, was not all that impressive. Based on conversations with then CUNY Chancellor Matthew Goldstein, who himself had served previously as the president of Baruch, it was agreed that the college should strive to further improve the composite academic achievement of its incoming first-year class, and we launched an effort to do precisely that.

Our first step was to model the demographic and academic characteristics of those applying for admission to determine how many applicants with certain specific academic qualifications (combined SAT scores and GPA) we would need to admit in order to achieve the desired improvement in the overall quality of the incoming class. We also were mindful, however, of Baruch's strong reputation for racial and ethnic diversity, and we made a firm decision *not* to improve student academic quality *at the expense* of maintaining a diverse class. Slowly, over several years, our efforts began to bear fruit. Table 5.1 indicates the improvement in mean combined SAT scores for each incoming first-year class between 2010 and 2020, which for the first time reached 1300 in 2020.[2]

To accomplish this significant improvement in the profile of its incoming first-year class, Baruch pioneered the use of econometric admissions modeling within CUNY, something that was already being done routinely at many other colleges and universities (and especially by private higher education institutions). To the best of my knowledge, Baruch remains one of the only schools in CUNY that engages in this kind of sophisticated admissions modeling. The results speak for

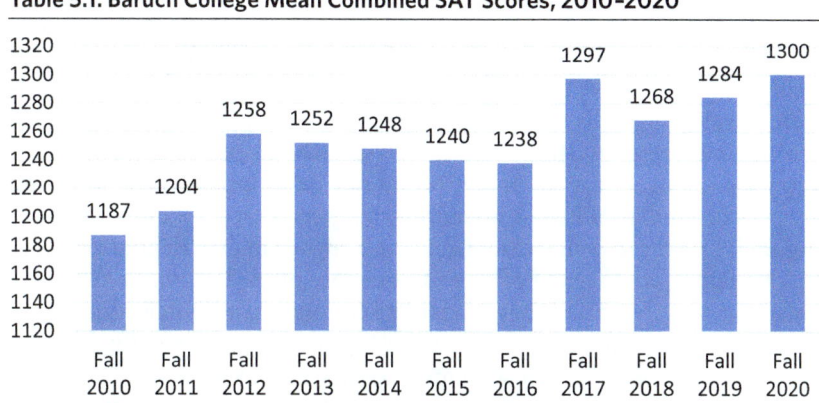

Table 5.1. Baruch College Mean Combined SAT Scores, 2010–2020

Fall 2010	Fall 2011	Fall 2012	Fall 2013	Fall 2014	Fall 2015	Fall 2016	Fall 2017	Fall 2018	Fall 2019	Fall 2020
1187	1204	1258	1252	1248	1240	1238	1297	1268	1284	1300

Source: Office of Enrollment Management, Baruch College, 2023

themselves; they indicate that students admitted to Baruch today are generally higher-performing, and many possess credentials that would have enabled them to be admitted to any number of the leading public universities and private colleges in the Northeast region. This improvement in academic quality has earned Baruch a "Very Selective" rating, with an admissions rate of 41%, according to the BestColleges.com and several other sources.[3]

SUPPORT FOR STUDENT SUCCESS

Perhaps the most distinctive feature of a Baruch College education is the comprehensive, "start to finish" academic support and enrichment made available to each student during their undergraduate career, whether that is 4 years, 6 years, or longer. While most colleges and universities, especially private institutions that charge much higher tuition, follow each student's progress and flag individuals for special attention when they appear to be struggling, Baruch has taken that process a step further. Given the financial limitations under which CUNY operates, the college has opted to use a portion of the private resources it raises to underwrite the cost of student-facing services, many of which are designed to help struggling students to succeed.

Thus, in addition to the usual advising services, Baruch's enrichment and support programs include (1) the Student Academic Consulting Center, which offers evaluation and tutoring services and weekly improvement workshops; (2) the Baruch College Writing Center, which provides free, professional writing support to currently enrolled undergraduate and graduate students; (3) the Bernard L. Schwartz Communication Institute, which helps students to become strategic, thoughtful communicators and creators, working with students in particular communication-intensive courses; (4) the Tools for Clear Speech program, which assists non-native English speakers (who make up a significant percentage of the Baruch student body) to achieve more effective and intelligible English communication, developing skills that empower them to succeed in their classrooms and their careers; and (5) the Starr Career Development Center, which provides inclusive career and professional development programs and services for undergraduate students and supports career readiness by helping each student to define career goals and engage in experiential learning.

As noted, while many of these services are offered routinely at *private* colleges and universities, they are far less common at resource-constrained PHEIs. Several of the programs enumerated above were actually designed specifically to assist Baruch students to overcome obstacles that might impede their academic progress toward graduation. For example, well more than half of Baruch undergraduates do not speak or write English as their native language. Thus, while they are smart and hard-working, they often need assistance to be able to perform at the level of native English speakers in their written and oral work. The ability to have full command of English is especially important in the world of business. The net result of this comprehensive, start-to-finish support effort is the highest year-over-year retention rate (88%) and the highest 4- and 6-year graduation rates (4-year rate: 40% and 6-year rate: 74%)[4] in the university, and both compare favorably on a national basis.

NEW ACADEMIC PROGRAMS AND INITIATIVES

Baruch has always had a strong reputation within CUNY as an academic innovator. In earlier years, when CUNY was more of a confederation of affiliated colleges than an integrated university, there was substantial latitude for departmental faculty to create new undergraduate curriculum and to develop new academic programs. As noted in Chapter 1, much of this flexibility was lost when CUNY implemented its Pathways initiative in 2013, because it required the standardization of undergraduate curriculum across the entire university. But even though this greater regimentation has limited Baruch's ability to offer its own *sui generis* undergraduate curriculum, it has not deterred the college from creating a significant number of new *graduate* programs in response to perceived needs. Below are some important examples of new academic initiatives implemented by each of Baruch's three schools.

The Zicklin School of Business: As the flagship business program in CUNY—and the only one offering both the MBA and PhD in Business—the Zicklin School of Business has continued to innovate academically at both the undergraduate and graduate levels. This has, in turn, helped to improve its high national ranking among public schools of business education. Among its recent graduate program innovations are the following:[5]

- **A new executive doctoral degree program.** The Zicklin Doctor of Business Administration degree is the first of its kind in the state of New York, offering senior business executives the opportunity to gain the skills needed to thrive in the C-suite or to broaden their opportunities as consultants. Some executives who are at the end of their professional career use the credential to enter clinical faculty positions. The program features a unique, multidisciplinary curriculum that employs a range of traditional and cutting-edge research methodologies structured

to accommodate executives' schedules with a limited number of on-campus residencies supported by online learning.
- **A new Master of Science degree in Business Analytics.** In the period between 2015 and 2018, big data and associated data analytics became essential technologies for businesses seeking competitive advantages in the increasingly competitive global economy and global supply chain. Many years of computerization of business processes and digitization of business data have resulted in the accumulation of mountains of digital data in organizations large and small. To make sense of the data and gain insights regarding consumers, products, markets, and technology, companies began hiring college graduates with training in data sciences and business functions. As a result, the demand for graduates in data analytics has skyrocketed. This master's degree program has become the fastest-growing in the history of the Zicklin School, with more than 200 students enrolled.
- **Innovations in the existing MBA program.** In the 2010–2020 decade, MBA programs across the country underwent major transformations because of the 2008 financial crisis and the subsequent Great Recession. Two trends emerged in the MBA education landscape: shorter curricula that enable students to do more internships during their program, and fully online programs that allow professional students to earn their MBA degree without having to give up their employment. Many business schools across the country revised their MBA curriculum by reducing the number of credits required for graduation, and some of the well-known MBA programs also began offering fully online MBA programs. The Zicklin School of Business responded swiftly to the changing landscape by launching a comprehensive redesign of the MBA program with a student-centric, career-oriented curriculum featuring a reduced number of credits to complete,[6] developing a fully online MBA program designed to serve the vast population of working professionals in the New York metropolitan region and beyond.
- **Development of eight dual-degree graduate programs with high-quality international institutions** in China, Italy, and Israel that take advantage of the Zicklin School's strategic location in New York City; its strong reputation in accounting, finance, and entrepreneurship; and its proximity to Wall Street. The school developed an innovative format for global graduate programs that has enabled international students to complete two degrees—one from their home institution and the other from the Zicklin School of Business.[7] These global dual-degree programs

have become some of the most impactful academic programs offered by the Zicklin School of Business.

The Weissman School of Arts and Sciences: Many people are surprised to learn that perhaps the most visible and prestigious graduate degree program at Baruch College, the master's degree in Financial Engineering (MFE), resides within the Weissman School of Arts and Sciences (rather than in the Zicklin School of Business). The reason is that the program was developed by the applied mathematics faculty in the Department of Mathematics. The MFE program prepares students for careers in the banking and financial industries, where its graduates develop the sophisticated investment algorithms that are used to do computerized stock trading. The program is extremely selective; only 8% of applicants are admitted, and students typically have undergraduate academic backgrounds in mathematics, physics, and economics. Graduates of the program are in high demand on Wall Street and elsewhere in the financial community, and after completing the program, students routinely receive six-figure salary offers.[8]

The MFE program has been ranked for many years as one of the top programs in the world, and it has occupied the #1 spot in QuantNet's annual ranking of Best Financial Engineering Programs for the past 3 years.[9] This ranking is based on a peer assessment, postgraduate employment rates, and student selectivity. Student teams from the MFE program also frequently win highly competitive, international trading competitions where they compete directly with students from similar programs based at elite, private institutions such as Princeton, MIT, Carnegie Mellon University, and the University of Chicago.

It is noteworthy that Baruch College is the home to this prestigious and top-ranked graduate program. Baruch's geographic advantage, given its location just a few miles north of Wall Street, together with its world-class business mathematics faculty and the highly competitive starting salaries that graduates receive, largely accounts for this salutary outcome.[10]

The Marxe School of Public and International Affairs: The Austin W. Marxe School of Public and International Affairs is New York City's only *public* graduate school dedicated to public administration and international affairs. It has been offering undergraduate and graduate degrees in public policy and administration since 1994. In 2017, a decision was taken to broaden the school's mission by initiating a new master's degree in International Affairs. The decision to undertake this significant step was based on three factors: (1) a market study that revealed significant interest in advanced international affairs training in a global city like New York; (2) an assessment that identified a notable lack of *affordable* graduate international affairs programs in the New York City metropolitan area; and (3) a recognition that such broadening of the school's academic focus would help to achieve its long-term strategic goals and maintain its competitiveness in the graduate academic market. New York City is, of course, home to the headquarters of the United Nations, as well as many global businesses and foundations, and more international nongovernmental organizations (INGOs) than any other city in the United States.

The challenges of creating and marketing an entirely new graduate degree program were not inconsiderable. First, the faculty of the Marxe School had to be convinced that adding such a program would advance the overall interests of the school and would not divert resources—including faculty lines—from existing academic programs. Second, the proposal had to be shepherded through the daunting maze of CUNY and state approvals, a process that required fully 2 years to complete. Third, decisions had to be made regarding how the degree program would be organized, including its major academic elements.[11] Fourth, new faculty had to be searched for and hired. Finally, a major marketing effort had to be organized to make potentially interested students aware of the program's existence. All of this was accomplished in time to admit an inaugural class in the fall of 2018, and the number of applications, admitted students, and enrolled students has increased steadily since then.[12]

INCREASING THE COLLEGE'S ENDOWMENT

Perhaps no other single factor better explains Baruch's academic quality, its financial stability, and its ability to recruit and retain faculty than its noteworthy annual success in private fundraising. The availability of these funds, which are not constrained in the same way that public "tax levy" dollars are, has been absolutely critical to sustaining the college's progress. It has enabled Baruch to augment budgets, to supplement salaries for key faculty, and to provide significant financial aid support for its students. It also has resulted in the naming and endowment of all three of Baruch's schools: the *Zicklin* School of Business, the *Weissman* School of Arts and Sciences, and the *Marxe* School of Public and International Affairs.[13] And it has enabled the college to raise the private funds needed to create a large outdoor plaza, a student center, and a state-of-the-art computing center and study lab, as well as many other facilities and programs.

For more than 50 years, the Baruch College Fund (BCF) has been the principal engine for this fundraising success. Begun in 1969 with an initial endowment gift from the college's namesake, Bernard M. Baruch, the BCF was formed shortly after Baruch became a fully independent senior college within the CUNY system, as an independent, private, nonprofit 501(c)(3) organization. It has grown from these modest beginnings to become an endowment (and quasi-endowment) fund that now approaches $300 million.

I am proud of the fact that during my tenure as president, the value of the BCF more than doubled. While some of this increase was due to strong financial market performance, it was also the result of highly successful management by its investment committee, which is composed of professional investors and portfolio managers, as well as several major new endowment gifts. This included the largest single gift in the college's history (and the second-largest in the history of CUNY), a $30 million endowment gift provided by Baruch alumnus Austin W. Marxe to name the School of Public and International Affairs.

Baruch derives a distinct advantage, from a fundraising standpoint, from the fact that its Zicklin School of Business is highly ranked among public university business schools. As previously noted, the majority of Baruch alumni attended the Zicklin School and many then went on to earn advanced degrees in business, which enabled them to achieve great success in the business world, and they were rewarded with substantial salaries and other forms of compensation that enabled them to give back to the college later in life. In fact, Zicklin alumni were responsible for naming and endowing *all three* of Baruch's schools. Unfortunately, most of the other CUNY senior colleges are not in a position to derive a similar benefit, and their fundraising and endowments reflect this fact.[14]

DEVELOPING MORE EFFECTIVE MANAGEMENT TOOLS TO IMPROVE FINANCIAL STABILITY

Because Baruch, like the rest of CUNY, is dependent on state support for much of its operating budget, it is highly vulnerable to the vagaries of the annual state budget process, as well as to exogenous financial and economic developments. So, for example, when state tax revenue dropped significantly during the Great Recession (December 2007–June 2009), the state of New York ordered both CUNY and SUNY to reduce their operating budgets right in the middle of the 2010–2011 academic year. In Baruch's case, this reduction amounted to about $6 million, which obviously had a significant negative impact on the operation of an already underresourced college.

Baruch recognized from the outset of the budget crisis that it was not possible—and certainly not desirable—to lay off academic or regular administrative staff,[15] meaning that we had to find other ways to cut such a large amount of money out of the budget *all at once* without negatively affecting academic operations. Ultimately, most of the cuts were absorbed through administrative cost reductions, such as reduced cleaning and maintenance, deferred capital purchases, and so on. But all new hiring, including the replacement of faculty who had retired or resigned, had to be suspended and administrative positions were left vacant. Fortunately, the state financial situation improved by the start of the next academic year, so some of these draconian cuts were avoided. But despite this, many of the impacts were felt for a long time thereafter—for example, until searches could be undertaken to hire new faculty and administrative staff in the lines that had been intentionally kept vacant.

Baruch took to heart the lessons of the 2010–2011 financial crisis. We recognized that this was not the first time, and surely would not be the last, that public "tax levy" revenues would be cut, and we understood that we needed to develop new strategies to cushion such financial shocks in the future to prevent negative impacts on the quality of Baruch's academic programs. Consequently, the college pursued a multifaceted plan to strengthen its overall financial position and to provide a financial "shock absorber." Some of the key elements of this strategy included the following:[16]

- **Enrollment:** Unlike many other CUNY colleges, Baruch has been able to maintain—and actually increase—its undergraduate enrollment. It was relatively easy for the college to open its admission gate a bit wider, since there was significant applicant demand at the undergraduate level. Increasing *graduate* enrollment proved somewhat more challenging, but Baruch has developed several new graduate degree programs as well as targeted executive master's degree programs that have helped to increase the number of graduate students.
- **Academic excellence fees:** Baruch pioneered the use of academic fees within the CUNY system, and it was the first to have such fees approved by the Board of Trustees. The introduction of such fees reflected the basic reality that some academic programs simply cost more to operate than others, and that additional revenue was needed to maintain the quality of the programs. CUNY had resisted recognizing this fact for many years, but given the pressure it always faces *not* to increase tuition, academic fees were the only viable alternative. The fees are typically quite modest (a few hundred dollars per student), and as per the CUNY board resolution, they can only be used to provide benefits and services directly to the students enrolled in a particular program. Baruch today has more academic excellence fees than any other CUNY college.
- **Vacancy savings policy:** After the 2010–2011 financial crisis, Baruch changed its policy from allowing each academic division to retain and use vacancy savings[17] for their own chosen purposes to a policy that required that vacancy savings revert to the general fund. So, for example, when a faculty or staff member departed, any savings resulting from the gap between their separation and a new hire would revert to the general fund.

Moreover, as part of the budget planning process, we required schools/divisions to set aside sufficient funds to cover all filled and authorized-but-unfilled positions at the beginning of the fiscal year. This policy change enabled the college to use freed-up funds more strategically, and to make sure that the funds were allocated to the highest-priority needs. Based on historical data, we were also able to project the amount of vacancy savings that would likely be achieved by the end of the year and then allocate these projected savings at the beginning of the new fiscal year to cover (or at least mitigate) the cost of so-called "mandatory needs"[18] or to absorb the impact of budget cuts or unexpected increases in budgeted expenses.

- **Position management:** We enforced the use of position management as a budget control tool. The first and most challenging step was to get the college's administrative staff to adopt the centralized university data system, known as CUNYFirst, as the *system of record* and stop maintaining various shadow systems on separate spreadsheets in each department. Without reliable and accurate data, we could not fully maximize the system's functionality for planning, analysis, and monitoring. Control of position management (i.e., adding new positions, changing the attributes of any currently vacant position, or eliminating positions that were no longer needed) was also shifted from Human Resources to the Budget & Planning office.

  A new policy was implemented stating that no search could be initiated unless there was an approved, vacant position number and funds committed to cover the cost. Although positions required approval in the past, we did not have an effective tool to monitor and enforce the rule until we started using position management. The process encouraged schools/divisions to actively review vacancies to set priorities and to deactivate positions that were no longer needed, thereby freeing up resources for higher-priority needs. Baruch was a leader within the CUNY system in using position management; many colleges did not use the tool in this manner and relied instead on their legacy procedures. CUNYFirst was not a perfect system by any measure, but it had utility for financial planning, and we used it.

- **Program review (old and new):** Along the same lines, we were able to conduct a financial review of all academic programs to identify those with declining demand and, therefore, producing less revenue. All new programs were required to submit a plan indicating that they could produce sufficient demand and showing that the revenue generated would cover costs.

- **Faculty hiring:** We formalized the approval process for faculty hiring to be better able to set priorities among competing requests. The provost, working closely with the deans, created a global list of all approved hires, rather than using the more fragmented, legacy process. Historical attrition data were used to create vacancy projections. But perhaps most importantly, replacement of department vacancies was no longer *automatic*, meaning that new hires are now approved based on enrollment and course demand. In effect, this eliminated the longstanding notion, which is common throughout academia, that faculty lines are permanent—that is, that they were "owned" by a given department and that when a faculty member retired or otherwise departed, the department assumed that it was *entitled* to replace that person in the same line without any consideration of the actual need for the specific expertise or demand for the courses.
- **Faculty salary supplements:** As noted previously, Baruch has used non–tax levy, private funds to provide annual salary supplements for key faculty, both as a recruitment and a retention tool. But the cost of these supplements has increased with each passing year, and the college's private investment resources have, at times, been seriously stretched. As a result, the Office of the Vice President for Administration and Finance undertook a thorough review of all endowment and quasi-endowment accounts to better utilize all available private funds. We also modestly increased the size of the fee charged for the management of the BCF private endowment funds both to have more funds available to cover administrative costs and to free up unrestricted funds to use for salary supplements. Finally, we were able to move some of the cost of the salary supplements to the tax-levy budget by persuading CUNY to allow changes in a faculty member's augmented salary.
- **Alternative revenue sources:** Additional revenue was derived from leasing space in the Baruch College Conference Center to external organizations. Charging for such external events enabled the college to cover the cost of *internal* college events—and over 85% of the events at the Conference Center are internal. The externally generated fees fully support the center staff and the maintenance of the space, while also providing a pool of discretionary funds for other college initiatives. Similarly, the college rents its athletic space and offers gym and swimming pool memberships to support our student athletic programs.
- **Energy savings:** Heretofore, the state of New York paid the cost of CUNY's utility bills. But the state implemented a change

in policy whereby it baselined the funds using historical cost calculations, and CUNY used the same historical numbers to provide each senior college with the funds to cover the cost of energy. A condition was added whereby, if the college spent *less* on energy, it could retain the cost savings, but if it spent *more* than the allocation, it had to cover the shortfall. Under this new incentive program, Baruch engaged in a series of aggressive energy-saving projects and initiatives, which produced significant positive results. It annually generated between $700,000 and $1 million in cost savings, which were used primarily to cover a sizable portion of the Buildings and Grounds budget, while the remaining cost savings went to the general fund.

NEW AND IMPROVED CAMPUS FACILITIES AND OUTDOOR SPACE

As noted in Chapter 4, like many other PHEIs across the country, the majority of Baruch's buildings are old and in need of modernization and renovation. Neither the state of New York, the city of New York, nor CUNY has the financial resources to address all of the needed capital improvements. Yet, the overall size of the college's undergraduate and graduate population has continued to increase, thereby putting additional strain on facilities to meet the expanded demand and near-constant usage. Baruch's student population was about 17,000 full-time students (undergraduate and graduate) when I arrived in 2010, but by the time I stepped down as Baruch president in 2020, the number had swelled to more than 19,000 students and was already on its way to the current 20,000 students. The college had to accommodate these additional students without the benefit of new space, since there were no funds available to lease (much less purchase) additional room.

Beyond the pressure of burgeoning student enrollment is the reality that many of the college's facilities are obsolescent and are being significantly overused, which means that they are often in disrepair or wearing out. For example, in some buildings the electrical and information technology (IT) infrastructure is not up to 21st-century standards and demands; science labs are out-of-date and inadequate; elevators are unreliable and frequently have to be taken out of service for repairs;[19] and hallways and classrooms often showed signs of wear and tear caused by near-constant use, despite the college's best efforts to maintain them.

During the decade from 2010 to 2020, the college was able to address some of its most urgent facilities problems and space needs. The decade-long efforts to close a single block of 25th Street in lower midtown Manhattan in order to build a protected pedestrian plaza and the ongoing (and excruciatingly slow) process of renovating the original Baruch College building at 17 Lexington Avenue were covered in the previous chapter. It's worth repeating, however, that the renovation of the college's original academic building may well require another *decade* (and possibly longer) to complete, given the glacial pace at which state capital funding is being provided.

On the other hand, the college has been able to use *private* funds to solve several other space-related needs, including the construction of a new student center, the renovation and expansion of its central computer lab, and the establishment of a multipurpose conference center that is used frequently by both private corporations and not-for-profit organizations in New York due to its flexible space and convenient location. The college's new main computer lab is a state-of-the-art, 263-seat facility that includes multimedia breakout rooms for student group projects. It is used heavily by Baruch students, many of whom cannot afford to purchase a computer to use in their homes.

Baruch's new student center is also an interesting example of a successful, symbiotic real estate relationship. The college had long been searching for additional space that could be used by the student government and other student organizations, because there was simply no remaining room in its existing buildings. At the same time, it was well known that the local Madison Square branch of the U.S. Post Office (USPS), which is located less than a block from the college, had ample space that it was no longer using due to the enormous reduction in the volume of "snail mail." After a number of years of fruitless discussions with the USPS in Washington, DC, a deal finally was struck[20] whereby the post office agreed to provide a long-term ground lease for the lower level of its Madison Square branch facility, and the college agreed to raise private funds to do the renovation and make upgrades.

This was clearly a "win-win" arrangement both for Baruch and for the USPS, and the result has been highly satisfactory for both parties. For Baruch students, the student center's location is very convenient, less than a two-minute walk from Baruch's main academic building, and the college activities in the building do not impede postal operations.

ACHIEVING STRONG NATIONAL AND REGIONAL RANKINGS

I presented data in Chapter 2 from two separate indices, one measuring social mobility and the other economic mobility, based on the experience of recent graduates of PHEIs across the country. Baruch ranks very highly on both scales, but especially so on the Social Mobility Index (SMI). The SMI measures the effectiveness of a particular college or university in enabling students from low-income families to move to well-paying jobs and overall social and economic success. For 6 consecutive years during the decade (2010–2020), Baruch College was ranked as the #1 college or university in the nation on the SMI. But it is not only on these social and economic mobility measures that Baruch has excelled. It also received high marks during this same time period from virtually every national and regional college/university ranking organization, including the following:[21]

- *U.S. News & World Report:* "Best Regional Universities-North"
  » #2 public institution in New York
  » #3 in the Northeast region
- *Money* magazine: "Best Colleges"
  » #1 public institution in New York
  » #5 among public colleges in the Northeast region
- *Forbes*: "America's Top Colleges"
  » #2 public institution in New York state
  » #1 public institution nationally for lowest student debt
- The Princeton Review: "Best Value Colleges"
  » #1 in the Northeast region; #8 in the U.S.
  » Top 20 best alumni networks in the U.S.
- *Washington Monthly:* "Best Bang for the Buck Colleges"
  » #7 public college in the Northeast region

In addition, the *New York Times* has published an "interactive ranking" in which Baruch was ranked fourth in the nation for "high earnings + low price," behind only Princeton University, MIT, and Stanford University (in that order), and #1 in the nation for "high earnings + low price + less selective."[22] While the value and accuracy of the algorithms underlying any of these rankings can always be questioned, taken collectively, they do indicate that Baruch performs very well against both public and private institutional peers and that it is seen as an extremely good *value* proposition with strong academic quality as well.

GROWING NATIONAL AND INTERNATIONAL VISIBILITY

Sometimes, of course, high rankings and other measures of success can have unintended—or at least, unanticipated—consequences. In Baruch's case, the number of undergraduate applications soared from 19,768 in 2014 to 24,307 in 2020. While there are many factors that likely contributed to this surge, Baruch's increased visibility in regional and national rankings and its reputation as a high-performing, good "bang for the buck" school are certainly both part of the explanation. Moreover, as I have contended here, the growing differential between the cost of private versus public higher education is driving (and will increasingly drive) more middle-class families to opt for public higher education for their students out of sheer economic necessity.

But the college's growing national and international visibility is about more than just rankings and affordability. It is also about academic quality, geographic location (in the heart of New York City), and career path access. Baruch increasingly is attracting students from beyond the New York metropolitan area, both nationally and internationally, who are interested in studying and living in New York City. They are drawn by the opportunity to obtain a quality education without having to assume substantial debt. But they are also attracted by the college's proximity to and connectivity with high-paying jobs in both the private and not-for-profit sectors in New York City. And it is a virtuous circle, because as the quality and ability of Baruch's graduates continues to increase and their preparedness for work on day one is noticed by employers, the college's alumni become even *more* desirable from a hiring standpoint.

CHAPTER 6

Does Baruch College Have a "Secret Sauce"?

BARUCH'S ADVANTAGEOUS POSITION WITHIN THE CUNY SYSTEM

Baruch is one of the five "senior colleges" within the CUNY system, each offering a comprehensive, 4-year, undergraduate curriculum and a range of graduate degree programs. The senior colleges are, in turn, among the 25 academic elements that make up The City University of New York. Some of the other senior colleges are considerably older than Baruch,[1] which was founded in 1968, and all of them have done, and continue to do, an admirable job educating primarily low-income students, many of whom might not otherwise be able to attend college. Indeed, there is little difference between the socioeconomic profiles of the students who enroll at Baruch and those who enroll at the other CUNY senior colleges. That said, Baruch's mean combined SAT score and GPA for its entering first-year students has been considerably higher for many years—in fact, they are the highest in CUNY other than for students who are enrolled in Macaulay Honors College. In addition, the CUNY colleges are essentially identical in terms of their tuition and fees, though total expenses may vary from campus to campus.

But Baruch does enjoy certain advantages in comparison to the other CUNY senior colleges. Clearly, one advantage is its physical location in the heart of midtown Manhattan.[2] The college is easily accessible by public transportation, and within walking distance of, or a short commute to, the headquarters of many large corporations, Wall Street, hundreds of not-for-profit organizations, and the United Nations. This proximity is very attractive to students, many of whom are attempting to juggle full-time work and full-time school. It also offers multiple opportunities for internships and an easy transition to full-time employment upon graduation.

All of this is relevant because, as discussed in earlier chapters, Baruch is home to the Zicklin School of Business. Zicklin students make up 71% of the Baruch undergraduate student body, and their academic capabilities (as measured by average SAT scores and GPAs) are typically well above average, both for Baruch and for CUNY as a whole. All students who are accepted to study at Baruch are subject to the same high standards, and all must have performed well in secondary school. But admission to the Baruch BBA degree program is a separate, more difficult process with even more rigorous standards; it requires a strong first-year GPA and the fulfillment of certain prerequisite courses (including a quantitative requirement). As a result, those who are admitted tend to be motivated and high performing, and once they matriculate, they rarely stop out.

Zicklin undergraduate business majors are strongly focused on completing their degrees as quickly as possible so that they can get out into the working world and begin generating income, both for themselves and for their families. Starting salaries for students graduating with a Zicklin School BBA degree are typically in the range of $60,000–$65,000, which in some cases may be more than the *combined* income of the student's entire family. As such, the first job after graduation is often a life-changing event.

Baruch business school graduates not only command significantly higher starting salaries, on average, than many of their fellow undergraduates, but they also go on to earn substantially more over the course of their professional careers. This means that they have larger lifetime giving capacity, and as noted in the previous chapter, this is reflected in the college's strong fundraising success over multiple decades—far greater than most of the other CUNY schools. While graduates of the Zicklin School of Business represent 71% of Baruch's alumni body, they account for about 90% of Baruch's Annual Fund and endowment fundraising.[3]

There are a number of other important factors that have enabled Baruch to be more academically successful and financially stable than its reference peer group within CUNY—or, for that matter, compared to many of its national peer PHEIs. Among these factors are the following:

- **Its mission:** While some might argue that the CUNY colleges all have essentially the same mission—namely, to educate the students of the city of New York (and beyond) irrespective of their financial circumstances—the reality is that Baruch's mission was at least somewhat different from the outset. As previously noted, until 1968 Baruch was part of The City College of New York, and it was often referred to by students and faculty alike as "City Downtown." Students studied on the "downtown" campus if they were pursuing a degree in either business or "civic administration" (which today is called public administration). Accounting and finance were two of the noteworthy strengths of the business program even in its early years. This meant that there was a natural process of self-selection in the makeup of its student body, although it was not unusual for students to start out in engineering or some other field of study on the "uptown" City College campus and later switch to business and move to the "downtown" campus.

- **Its students:** Like the rest of CUNY, the typical profile of many Baruch undergraduates is first- (or second-) generation immigrant and deeply connected to their (often recently arrived) immigrant families. Such students can often be intimidated by a system that they are determined to join but do not yet feel fully a part of or completely knowledgeable about how to navigate. Indeed, many of the brightest students in this cohort likely could have obtained full-ride scholarships and living expenses at other colleges and universities, both public and private, including many outside of the New York City area; but they feared they might feel alien and alone in such a setting. Baruch, on the other hand, is a place where they can get elite-level support, but their fellow students share a similar background and there are few reminders of income disparity on campus.[4] Attending Baruch also permits them to remain physically close to their families and ethnic communities.

  Though every bit as economically challenged as the students enrolling elsewhere in CUNY, Baruch students have tended to be (a) more career-focused, (b) more highly motivated to excel academically, and (c) more dedicated to the expeditious completion of their degrees. And this is borne out by Baruch's high completion rate. There may be a number of reasons for this, including the fact that (as previously noted) the majority of Baruch undergraduates are pursuing business degrees. But it may also be related to the students' immigrant backgrounds and the unwavering focus of their families—especially in the Asian community—on the values of hard work and educational advancement.[5]

- **Its faculty:** Baruch's academic reputation and the opportunity to teach and work in the heart of New York City have consistently attracted a highly capable and diverse faculty. They have trained in some of the top doctoral programs in the United States and around the world, and many have taught and done research in other top universities and colleges before joining the Baruch faculty.

  As previously noted, business faculty are more highly compensated than those in the liberal arts or public affairs, which makes recruiting and retaining them a constant challenge. But business faculty typically are attracted by the multiple consulting opportunities in New York, and they can also use this outside support to supplement their income and to underwrite the cost of their research. These advantages have occasionally been a source of tension within the broader Baruch faculty, where people are well aware of the salary disparities. But it is important to emphasize that such pay differentials reflect market signals; they are not an indication of "bias" regarding the salary decisions made by the college.

- **Its higher expectations:** Because Baruch has only been a CUNY senior college for the past 55 years, it may have benefited from generally more rigorous academic standards than were previously the case within CUNY. Following the end of the disastrous open admissions experiment (discussed in Chapter 1)—which had such negative ramifications for the university, both in terms of its academic reputation and its ability to recruit and retain quality faculty—the general inclination was to move in the *opposite* direction, namely, to demand academic rigor and accountability. Baruch was fortunate in that its academic reputation did not suffer to nearly the same extent during the open admissions period as happened at the other senior colleges. This may have been a fortunate result of the fact that Baruch's primary mission was educating students for careers in business and public affairs, both of which required strong quantitative and analytic skills. These requirements were *not* relaxed during the open admissions period. Thus, the norms of academic rigor, strong student academic achievement, and faculty productivity have always been engrained in the culture of the college, and they have only deepened over time.

- **Its different approach to internal and external political issues:** Universities are generally places where strong and often opposing political views, sharp discourse, and open intellectual disagreement are welcome, encouraged, and protected. This is as it should be; it is the very essence of academic freedom and entirely in keeping with the principles of an open university. As the largest urban university in the United States, and one that is inextricably intertwined with the people of the city of New York, CUNY has long been known as a place where both students and faculty frequently exercised their right of free speech and engaged in peaceful disagreement and protest on a myriad of issues, both internal and external to the institution. And during the past few decades, there has been no lack of political issues on which students and faculty alike have argued and often disagreed.

Many of these issues have focused on *internal* CUNY policies and financial decisions. Clearly, the issue that has received the most extensive and acrimonious debate has been the continuing need for modest tuition increases, which have been driven by the failure to obtain needed increases in state support. This situation reached its apex during the administration of Andrew Cuomo, when there were years in which CUNY received little or no increase in its state budget allocation, leaving the university with little choice but to raise tuition simply in order to maintain existing academic operations. This led to increasingly vehement protests on many of the CUNY campuses, with some demanding a return to the policy of "tuition-free" undergraduate education that had ended more than 30 years ago. While free higher education is undoubtedly a laudable goal, in today's economy, and within the existing state tax revenue and budget constraints, a return to free higher education is completely unattainable and unrealistic, from both a political and financial standpoint.

Beyond the world of internal CUNY politics, there often has been strong debate across a wide range of *external* "hot button" issues, which have included, for example, alleged covert NYPD surveillance of Muslim students on the CUNY campuses following the 9/11 terrorist attacks, the rights of the Palestinians in the Middle East and how these issues are taught and discussed on some of the campuses, and anti-Semitism and racism in all its forms. Yet it is a curious fact, however, that neither internal nor external political issues have played a significant role on the Baruch campus. Only a relatively small number of students and faculty are politically active at Baruch; most remain focused on teaching and learning and the completion of their academic degrees.

It is difficult to identify a single reason why the situation on the Baruch campus differs so much from the other CUNY colleges. But here as well, it may be related to the large number of business students enrolled at the college, who tend to be singularly career-focused, and a faculty more interested in teaching, research, and writing than in engaging in political protest. Also, because the faculty of the Zicklin School of Business tend to be more highly compensated than others at the university, they may be less inclined than their counterparts to engage in protest about salary-related matters.

- **Its limited union activism:** Given that New York has a reputation as a "union-friendly" city, it makes sense that CUNY would have a long history of union activism. As discussed previously, the Professional Staff Congress (PSC) represents all CUNY faculty and most staff,[6] and all compensation and workplace matters are addressed through collective bargaining at the university level—meaning that the individual colleges have only limited influence in these decisions.

Many of the CUNY campuses do have strong and active PSC chapters with many members who mobilize, and often demonstrate, during the budget season, demanding more resources from the state and from CUNY and calling for higher wages each time the union contract is up for renewal. Given the sometimes fraught relationship between the state government and CUNY, the PSC has been an important voice advocating for the needs (and rights) of CUNY faculty and staff. That said, while the PSC has had some notable accomplishments, the union has sometimes been unable to achieve its objectives, and there have been periods when faculty and staff have had to work without a contract.

Union activism has proven to be an important element in the broader effort to advance the interests of PHEIs in New York. But unions also have a downside. Their "work to the rules" approach and occasional resistance to change—for example, on issues such as teaching loads, use of hybrid and remote formats, and faculty scholarly output—can slow efforts to modernize and streamline academic programs and curriculum, which often makes unionized institutions less flexible and less competitive.

Here as well, Baruch has been an outlier; union activism has been generally limited on the campus. While there is a small contingent of union-active faculty, the majority do not participate, preferring to be left to pursue their research and teaching. There are even some who are explicitly anti-union and do not participate as a matter of principle. Generally speaking, union activism on the CUNY campuses seems to be focused primarily in the liberal arts faculties, where salaries are lower. Faculty appointed in the Zicklin School of Business and the Marxe School of Public and International Affairs appear to have less interest in or affinity with the PSC union and its agenda. Faculty in both schools also have outside consulting and other professional relationships that enable them to augment their CUNY salaries. Thus, they may be less invested in the PSC's efforts to gain increases in compensation and benefits.

- **Its successful and sustained private fundraising:** One of the principal reasons that Baruch has been able to overcome (or at least, mitigate) many of the obstacles that obstruct or slow progress at the other CUNY colleges, as well as at many other public colleges and universities across the country, has been its ability to generate significant private support. As noted in Chapter 4, Baruch's private fundraising foundation, the Baruch College Fund (BCF), has achieved great success over the past few decades. Since 2003, the BCF has raised at total of $370 million in annual operating support, endowment gifts, and planned gifts, and the size of the Baruch endowment has increased from $139 million to $296 million during this same period.[7]

Here as well, Baruch has a distinct advantage within CUNY due to the fact that so many of its students enroll in and graduate from the Zicklin School of Business. Even with only the undergraduate BBA degree, Zicklin alumni often earn considerably higher salaries and, therefore, have larger annual and lifetime giving capability. There are even a few billionaires, and many millionaires, among the Baruch alumni body. While this obviously makes it easier for the college to achieve its fundraising goals, it does not entirely explain why Baruch has been so much more successful in acquiring private resources.

Over the past decade, the BCF has generated average annual fund support of $2.5 million–$3 million, and its annual gala dinner typically raises more than $1 million. These numbers may appear modest when compared to the average endowment and annual fundraising totals achieved at the leading *private* higher education institutions, but they are considered very respectable within the context of public higher education. In 2021, annual giving to public universities and colleges was approximately $20 billion, but the percentage of alumni actively contributing was only 22.9%, as compared to the percentage of alumni contributing to private universities, where the annual participation rate was 53%.[8] The rate of individual giving to public universities and colleges has always been substantially lower than alumni giving to private colleges and universities, but as state support has failed to keep pace with rising costs, this gap becomes increasingly significant.

I described earlier the success of the BCF in increasing the college's endowment and providing a strong and reliable flow of annual operating revenue that can be used to supplement the New York state "tax levy" resources. These private dollars have enabled the college to address a variety of needs that its CUNY peer institutions and other public colleges simply cannot. Baruch has been able to make of its private funds for (a) a variety of academic enrichment programs to accelerate and enhance student achievement, (b) supplementation of the salaries of high-performing faculty both to recruit and retain them,

and (c) development of new physical facilities to enhance the environment for teaching and learning.
- **Its substantial on-campus engagement with private companies and nonprofit organizations:** Yet another obvious benefit derived from Baruch's standing as the premier business school in the CUNY system and its convenient geographic location is that it has enabled the college to cultivate relationships with many large private corporations based in New York City, including the leading banks, investment firms, and so on. The Zicklin School of Business regularly invites corporate leaders to campus to give talks and to participate in seminars, and employees from dozens of New York companies participate in Baruch's "Executives on Campus" program, where they mentor students who are preparing to enter the business world.[9]

  In addition, New York–based companies have increasingly come to see Baruch as a fertile ground for recruiting.[10] In fact, CUNY graduates make up a significant percentage (10%) of the new hires in New York City and New York state's workforce. From 1991 to 2020, about 850,000 CUNY graduates were employed in the state in both the private and public sectors.[11] Thus, companies have recognized that they have a vested interest in helping to sustain the college and its programs in order to maintain the quality and quantity of potential applicants in the hiring pipeline. A few companies even make annual financial gifts from their corporate foundations in support of the Zicklin School and its students.

  During the past 2 decades, not-for-profit organizations have also begun to engage actively on the Baruch campus. Like the representatives of the corporate world, the leaders of these organizations are invited to campus to give talks and to participate in seminars, primarily at the Marxe School of Public and International Affairs, and they too participate in the "Executives on Campus" program. Not-for-profit organizations are alsoactively interested in recruiting Baruch students, especially those graduating with MPA degrees. They offer internship opportunities and actively recruit on campus. While they do not have the financial capacity to make annual gifts, they nevertheless support the Marxe School in other ways, and the work they do is of substantial interest to many Baruch faculty and students.
- **Its comprehensive, start-to-finish academic support and enrichment:** As discussed in Chapter 5, Baruch's comprehensive, start-to-finish academic support and enrichment programs provide support that is not found to the same extent in many

other PHEIs. The college has opted to use a portion of the private resources that it raises each year to underwrite the cost of services that assist struggling students to succeed so they not fall between the cracks.

DOES BARUCH *HAVE* A "SECRET SAUCE"?

I have identified in this chapter a range of factors that provide Baruch College with significant advantages, advantages that many schools in its peer reference group do not enjoy. But the question remains: Do these factors, even when taken together, support the argument that the college has developed a unique approach that has enabled it to succeed and to become a highly ranked positive outlier, when many of its peer PHEIs continue to struggle financially and, in some cases, academically? After examining this question closely while working on this volume, I conclude that the answer to this question is *no*, Baruch does *not* possess a "secret sauce" or recipe for success. In fact, I have found no evidence to support the notion that either the executive leadership of the college since it became independent in 1968 or the faculty and staff ever pursued an explicit strategy to position Baruch to be more successful than its peers.

That said, it is undeniable that despite the continued inadequacy of public funding from the state of New York, the many challenges of operating a college with more than 20,000 students in aging and inadequate facilities, and the academic and bureaucratic constraints imposed by the CUNY bureaucracy, Baruch has found a way to continue to succeed and even to prosper. The factors identified earlier in this chapter go a long way toward explaining this "positive deviance." Beyond that, I conclude that it is likely a fortuitous combination of luck, perspicacity, and deeper private financial pockets that explains the college's success.

As I have noted, Baruch is a considerably younger institution than the other four CUNY senior college, so it began its existence less burdened by the historical baggage and limitations that these institutions have carried for many decades. In fact, it is not hyperbolic to state that Baruch identifies with—and measures itself against—a different academic reference group than do its CUNY peers. This group includes the best public—and many excellent private—universities and colleges in the Northeast region and beyond. And the academic quality of Baruch's students over the years—and perhaps more importantly, their significant professional accomplishments and upward social and economic mobility—appears to support the college's pursuit of such high standards and expectations.

CHAPTER 7

Is the Baruch "Model" Sustainable and Replicable?

WHAT EXPLAINS BARUCH'S ACADEMIC SUCCESS AND FINANCIAL STABILITY?

In the previous chapter, I suggested that Baruch was in many respects a positive outlier, or "positive deviant." Although it struggles with most of the same problems as other PHEIs across the country—for example, lack of adequate, annual public tax levy support, aging and obsolescent facilities, and pressure to admit an increasing number of students who cannot afford the cost of attending private colleges and universities—the college has managed to stay on track academically and to develop new undergraduate and graduate programs, while somehow remaining financially stable.

Data were presented in Tables 3.2a and 3.2b on 14 other successful PHEIs in six states across the country that have academic and financial profiles roughly similar to that of Baruch. It is obvious from an analysis of that data that Baruch is by no means the *only* successful PHEI. But a detailed comparison of these peer institutions reveals that Baruch also performs well across almost *all* the categories analyzed, including both social and economic mobility indexes and price-to-earnings premium. The college has one of the lowest tuition rates and the largest number of Pell-eligible students among all of the institutions included. In fact, Baruch is a national leader in enrolling Pell-eligible students. So, it can be stated that Baruch does represent a successful model for public higher education, even if it does not possess a "secret sauce" explaining its success. I will address subsequently the question of whether it is also a *replicable* model.

As I noted in Chapter 6, it is interesting to speculate on whether when Baruch College was established as an independent senior college in 1968, there was any intention to make it a model for public higher education. It was already the case that the college was enrolling high-achieving students, particularly in business; but there is nothing in the historical record to indicate that those responsible for the decision to separate CCNY and Baruch were thinking about creating some sort of new and *different* educational paradigm. In fact, CUNY was at that time still pursuing its disastrous open admissions experiment, and the New York City financial crisis was approaching, which would result in a major retrenchment at CUNY. So, all things considered, it seems highly unlikely that the New York City Board of Higher Education[1] *intended* to pursue a different educational model when it approved the establishment of Baruch College.

It is also worth considering the extent to which Baruch's success can be tied to the role of public higher education in the state of New York, which dates back to the founding of the Free Academy in New York City in 1847[2] and similar academic institutions in key upstate cities.[3] Due to the high concentration of *private* colleges and universities in the state, and in the Northeast more generally, New York may have seen less need to invest in public education than did states in other parts of the country. This, in turn, may explain why the State University of New York (SUNY) was not formally established until 1948 and CUNY not until 1961, and it also may provide insight as to why neither university has ever emerged as the state flagship university, as happened in many other states (especially the "land grant" state universities).[4]

Nevertheless, given the enormous number of immigrants who were flooding into New York between the middle of the 19th and 20th centuries, there was a desire to provide this arriving immigrant population with the education that would enable them to participate in and contribute to the city and state economy. And this was actually the primary stated rationale for the creation of the Free Academy. New York City has, of course, always been the "melting pot" of America, and most of those coming from other parts of the world arrived near-penniless; and therefore lacking the capacity to *pay* for education of any kind.

But none of this early history explains the success during the past few decades of modern-day Baruch College. There are substantial similarities in the academic organization, curriculum, and tuition charged by the five CUNY senior colleges. But it was also the case, as I previously noted, that the four "legacy" senior colleges (CCNY, Hunter, Brooklyn, and Queens) were more severely affected by the open enrollment period than was Baruch. The result was that these schools lost some of their best faculty and suffered a significant reputational impact and a decline in student enrollment, which had, in turn, a deleterious effect on their financial condition. Baruch College was not affected in the same way or to the same extent, however, because it did not relax or eliminate its admissions standards and academic requirements.

In fact, as I have suggested earlier in this volume, the most important factor explaining Baruch College's academic success and its financial stability can be found in the nature of its original academic mission—namely, the education of students for careers in business and government.

Even though, today, the college has a far broader academic mission, with well-qualified and respected faculties of Arts & Sciences and of Public & International Affairs, it remains the case that about 71% of graduating seniors each year receive the BBA degree.

The Baruch faculty has gone to great lengths to make sure that all students receive a broad exposure to the liberal arts, though this was not always the case. Indeed, some have argued that the primary factor explaining Baruch's "positive outlier" status was that, for many decades, it offered what amounted to a "vocational" business curriculum that primarily trained students for rapid assimilation into the business world without preparing them adequately for their future role as citizens.[5]

While I think this is a historically accurate observation, it does not reflect the actual curricular requirements that Baruch students have been required to fulfill in recent decades. In fact, all of Baruch's business majors must now take a liberal arts minor in the Weissman School of Arts and Sciences. Half of the credits required for the Bachelor of Business Administration (BBA) degree focus on the arts, sciences, and general education in order to provide graduates with a solid and broad educational foundation. And the business curriculum itself exposes students to ethical values that encourage participation in community affairs and an awareness of the relationship between business and the legal, political, and social settings in which it functions. The liberal arts minor consists of three courses of disciplinary study (and in some instances, interdisciplinary study), and it also includes a capstone course that is research-oriented and communication-intensive.[6]

As I have previously observed, undergraduates in the Zicklin School of Business are typically high-performing students who are eager to complete their degree as quickly as possible. When they do so, they are offered sufficiently high starting salaries that they are able to pay off their educational debt fairly quickly. Thus, Baruch's high national and regional rankings as a "Best Value" institution, as well as its #1 national ranking in the Social Mobility Index, can be explained by a straightforward combination of low tuition cost, the accumulation of little or no debt, strong academics, and relatively high compensation upon graduation.

CAN THE BARUCH COLLEGE "MODEL" BE REPLICATED ELSEWHERE?

To argue that Baruch College is a "model" for public higher education may somewhat overstate the case. In fact, some of the factors that have contributed to the Baruch's success are either exogenous to the college or occurred for other reasons. For example, Baruch's low tuition is primarily the result of the historical fact that, for many years, CUNY charged no tuition at all. Until the New York City financial crisis of the late 1970s, all of the CUNY colleges were tuition-free for everyone, and this philosophical approach has carried over into the present day in the CUNY Board's general disinclination to raise tuition, unless there is simply no economic alternative.[7] The state of New York also plays a role in the setting of tuition rates, since the tuition increases proposed by the CUNY and SUNY boards must be approved in Albany. The net result, over time, has consistently been one of the lowest in-state tuition rates in the country.

This is not to suggest, however, that CUNY students are happy with or readily accept the slow, continuing rise in tuition, however modest. Many have been quite outspoken about the fact that they believe tuition is too high and that CUNY is becoming unaffordable for those living on limited resources. Some have advocated for a return to tuition-free education, but they have never offered a politically coherent or economically viable strategy for achieving this outcome.

The state of New York provides another benefit to low-income students: the Tuition Assistance Program (TAP). TAP helps economically eligible New York residents pay tuition at approved schools in the state, which of course includes both CUNY and SUNY. An annual TAP award can be as much as $5,665, and because TAP is a grant, it does not need to be repaid. Thanks to the existence of TAP, students from families with a combined income below a specified amount (currently set at $110,000) can complete an undergraduate degree without having to pay any tuition if they stay on track to graduate. While TAP is not unique on a national basis, there are few other states that make it possible for low-income students to attend college tuition-free.

The factors internal to Baruch that have made it such an attractive educational option were analyzed in Chapters 5 and 6. To summarize, the following are among the most important of these:

- Extremely low tuition, combined with access to the New York State Tuition Assistance Program for low-income families.
- High admission standards (relative to the rest of CUNY) that produce high-performing students.
- The presence of a highly ranked business school, with students eager to complete their degree and get out into the working world.
- An ethnically and racially diverse student body with international origins in more than 150 countries.
- A variety of privately financed, cocurricular programs offering comprehensive, start-to-finish academic support for undergraduate students.
- A strategic location in the heart of lower midtown Manhattan with easy access to public transportation and close to many potential employers.

- Substantial, long-term private fundraising success that has enabled the college to hire and retain key faculty through salary augmentation and to offer substantial private financial aid.

All of this begs the question of whether these factors, taken together, constitute a "Baruch model" of public higher education, and if so, whether the model is replicable by other PHEIs. As I stated in Chapter 6, I am not prepared to argue that Baruch has developed a *sui generis* formula, compared with other PHEIs, that has enabled it to succeed and prosper while many other public institutions have struggled. But an analysis of the factors enumerated above suggests that Baruch *does* have certain advantages that may be difficult for other institutions to fully replicate.

It is worth focusing a bit further on the advantages that Baruch derives from having the flagship business school for the CUNY system. In fact, for many years Baruch's business program was the *only* business school in CUNY, which gave it an obvious leg up. This is no longer the case, however, as there are now three business schools in the system.[8] But this seems reasonably appropriate, given the apparently inexhaustible demand for business graduates in the New York metropolitan area, especially since two of the schools teach only undergraduates. At this writing, the Zicklin School of Business remains the *only* program within the CUNY system that offers the MBA and PhD degrees in business. It would be a *serious* mistake, in my view, if the other two colleges offering business programs were permitted to compete in either of these graduate degree arenas, since that would unquestionably dilute the market.[9]

I have previously explained the various ways that having the business program has helped the college, both in the immediate and longer term (i.e., as its alumni rise to more senior and better remunerated positions). These same advantages would, in principle, also accrue to other PHEIs with well-regarded business programs. Indeed, the same or similar advantages could be derived by schools that offer degrees in other professional disciplines, such as engineering, medicine, or law, since they all produce alumni who typically go on to have more highly remunerated careers. Medicine and law are only available, however, at the *graduate* level, which reduces to some degree their beneficial alumni giving impact.

It is the case, of course, that many of the other 14 PHEIs included among reference institutions examined in Chapter 3 have *other* advantages and features, including attractive campuses, residential living facilities, and large collegiate athletic programs, that Baruch does not possess. But none has been quite as successful as Baruch in attracting high-performing students, graduating large numbers of them on time and with little or no debt, and having them move directly into well-paying jobs.

This leads to the conclusion that there is nothing that would prevent other PHEIs from successfully emulating the "Baruch model," but these other institutions would need to be prepared to commit significant additional financial resources to develop degree programs (if they don't already have them) in business, engineering, or possibly in other STEM disciplines, and to develop a holistic approach to student advancement, especially for students from economically and socially challenged backgrounds who are dealing with multiple economic, family, and work challenges.

THE FUTURE SUSTAINABILITY OF THE "BARUCH MODEL"

Baruch's prospects for sustaining its leading role among comparable PHEIs appear reasonably good. There would seem little reason to anticipate a dramatic change in its academic profile or financial stability. That said, there are always "unknowns" that create uncertainty about the future. First and foremost, it is impossible to know what the state of New York will do in the coming years regarding the level of its financial support for public higher education, and for CUNY in particular. While there is currently no reason to anticipate that the state will enact significant reductions in its annual support for CUNY and SUNY, the possibility cannot be entirely ruled out. Much will depend on the health and availability of state tax revenues, which is determined by a variety of factors, including the overall status of the national and state economies, the wealth of New York state's residents, and the other competing priorities (and their urgency and political salience).

Table 7.1 shows how the state of New York compares nationally in terms of its financial support for public higher education. The good news is that New York ranks third in the nation at the present time in terms of its total budgetary commitment. It is noteworthy that while New York compares favorably with the state of Texas, the #1 ranked state, California, commits more than twice as many tax dollars to public higher education as either of these other two states. Of course, California also has the largest population of the three. In recent years, many states have pressed their state-supported universities to diversify their sources of financial support—and some have required their PHEIs to significantly raise tuition, especially for out-of-state students, as a way of relieving budgetary pressures.[10]

A second unknown for Baruch is whether it will be able to sustain the same level of *private* fundraising in the coming years. As I noted in Chapter 4, the demographic mix of the college has changed/is changing rather dramatically. Whereas 30 years ago Jewish students made up the largest share of the student body, today Asian students have the largest representation, and there are substantially greater numbers of Latino and African American students than there were in previous years. This

Table 7.1. A Comparison of State Support of Public Higher Education, 2018

State Support 2018

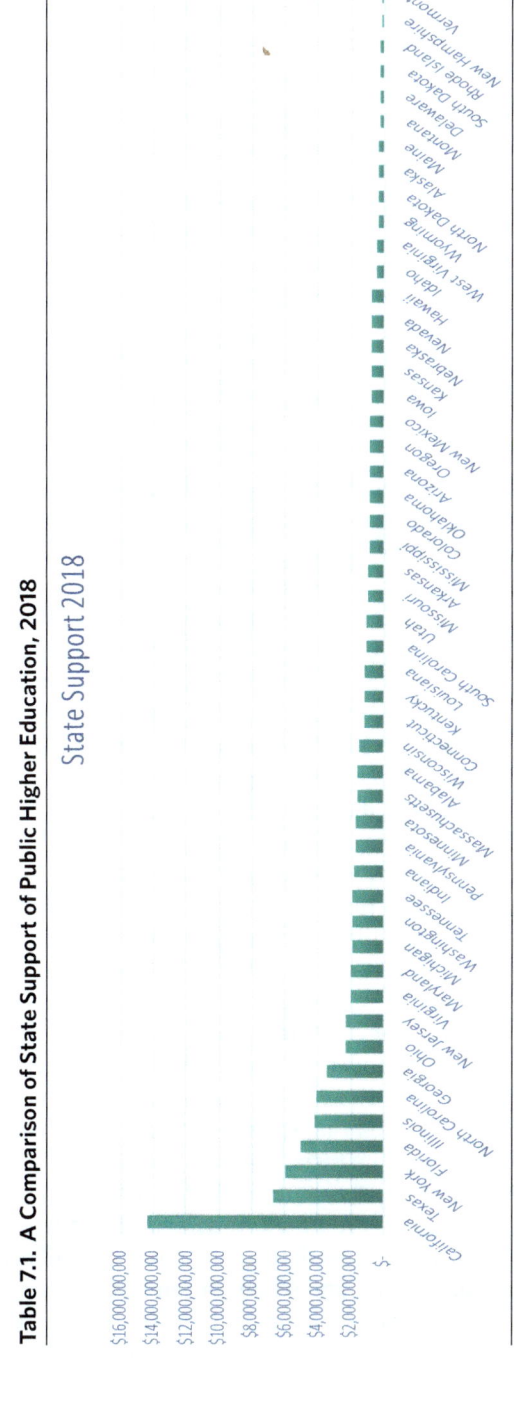

Source: State Higher Education Executive Officers Association, Grapevine National Table 3, FY 2018.

is altogether a *good* thing; it is a sign that the Baruch "dream machine" remains dynamic and has become accessible to a much broader and more diverse cross-section of the population. But it is far from certain that alumni from these other ethnic and racial communities will step up to sustain the same level of annual private giving, and whether they will be willing and able to continue the tradition of making significant testamentary and endowment gifts.

There are many successful Asian, African American, and Latino people in New York City who have given generously within their own communities. What remains unclear, however, is whether they can be convinced to give in large numbers and at high levels to a *state-supported* institution like Baruch. Should this support fail to materialize, it would have a very significant, negative impact on the college's ability to sustain programmatic excellence, to continue to provide private financial aid support, and to hire and retain outstanding faculty, especially in the business school.

A third unknown is how CUNY itself will evolve in the coming years. The university is unique in the U.S. academic context, given that it operates 25 separate campuses with more than 240,000 full-time students, undergraduate and graduate, all within 15 miles of one another. Due to this geographic proximity, there has been a continuing effort by the CUNY Chancellery (particularly since the end of the open admissions era), driven in part by pressure from the state government in Albany, to exert significantly greater centralized control over what was originally a loose confederation of colleges by standardizing curriculum and administrative procedures and by exerting greater oversight over academic, financial, and management matters more generally.

To be fair, at least some of this pressure to centralize was and is warranted—and, in fact, was probably long overdue. But some of it was the result of a natural bureaucratic tendency to attempt to consolidate control and enforce uniformity on all of constituent elements of an institution—whether or not that control is practicable or even called for. As noted, some of the impetus is the result of political pressure and criticism that has come from the state, especially during the years when Andrew Cuomo served as governor. And it is true that there have been a number of financial scandals and other management problems that arose during the 2010–2020 period that caused the state to demand greater accountability and improved financial controls.

In Baruch's case, the requirement to conform has been especially problematic because its strong enrollment and favorable financial condition have positioned it to do more—that is, to innovate new academic programs, to expand curriculum, and so on. But in recent years, the college's ambition has been constrained by the often-stifling nature of CUNY's many rules and requirements, some of which appear to lack a solid basis in state (or city) law or regulation. (Some have suggested that many of these rules are largely based on "folklore" that has been handed down but is lacking a modern legal rationale.) Unfortunately, the inevitable result of centralization and outmoded and overreaching rules and regulations is a regression to the "lowest common denominator" across the university.

Too often, for a variety of reasons the CUNY Chancellery has been unwilling to permit and encourage individual initiative by the colleges or to reward excellence. Instead, it has chosen, at least publicly, to act as if all of the university's constituent elements are essentially of *equal* quality and productivity—or, as I have put it elsewhere, that "all of the children are equal and must be treated as such." Clearly, this is not and cannot realistically be the case, and there is an *urgent* need for CUNY to change its approach.

The truth of the matter is that CUNY's continuing inability or unwillingness to recognize that all the colleges are *not* equal in their academic quality, their actual performance (meaning the quality and number of students they enroll *and graduate*), or in their financial situation—and to act on this reality—will have an increasingly deleterious and disruptive effect on the university in the years to come. In Baruch's case, it will likely limit the college's ability to innovate and to continue to move forward, especially if other elements of the university are struggling to maintain enrollment and to stabilize their finances.

CHAPTER 8

Reflections on the Future of Public Higher Education

THE CHALLENGES FACING HIGHER EDUCATION IN GENERAL

Much has been written in recent days about the challenges facing higher education.[1] There is demonstrable evidence that the pandemic and its aftermath have wreaked havoc, especially on small, private, nonprofit institutions, many of whom were already teetering on the brink of insolvency. These colleges have continued to struggle financially even as the pandemic has faded, due to a lack of enrollment and insufficient endowment resources. Just since the start of the pandemic in 2020 alone, 13 private, nonprofit colleges have shut down in the United States,[2] and a number of others have been forced to merge. And PHIEs have felt the effects as well, with many experiencing significant enrollment declines, especially the nation's community colleges.

Just as this volume was being completed, for example, there were numerous reports in the media regarding the plans announced at West Virginia University, the publicly funded university in the state of West Virginia, to cut 169 faculty positions and eliminate 30 degree programs, including *all* of its foreign language courses.[3] There apparently were a number of reasons why this university found it necessary to undertake such draconian measures, including current (and expected future) declines in enrollment, which were projected to result in a $45 million deficit, along with a general decline in student interest in certain liberal arts disciplines. The enrollment decline at West Virginia was accelerated by the pandemic, with the university experiencing an 8% drop since 2020.[4] There is also serious doubt about the willingness or capacity of the state of West Virginia to provide the additional funds needed to deal with a deficit of this size.

West Virginia University is not alone in this regard; a number of other publicly supported universities are confronting the same or similar challenges. Penn State University, for example, reported that it faced a $63 million deficit in 2023, despite having instituted a hiring freeze and other cost savings, and Rutgers University, the state university of New

Jersey, was forced to slash budgets and raise tuition to help close a $77 million deficit.[5] CUNY was not entirely spared either. During the pandemic years, the university imposed strict hiring controls and a spending freeze, due to significant declines in enrollment that caused a drop in tuition revenue. Baruch College was, in fact, the *only* CUNY college that did not suffer any enrollment decline during the pandemic.

There are also, of course, a number of *new* challenges facing the nation's higher education system, including, among others: (a) how to cope with the demographic decline in the number of college-ready young people, (b) how to integrate and manage both face-to-face and virtual online learning, (c) how to deal with generative AI and its implications for teaching and learning, and (d) how to deal with—and push back against—conservative attempts to "reform" higher education by eliminating and/or defunding certain curricula, banning books, and censoring faculty at state-supported institutions who teach or speak publicly about certain subjects. In addition, the recent Supreme Court decision that ended race-based affirmative action admissions—and a likely future challenge to legacy admissions[6]—is likely to be highly disruptive, especially for private institutions that are seeking to achieve a more diverse student body.

Beyond the effect of the pandemic, much of the drop in enrollments suffered at private, nonprofit, and publicly supported educational institutions can be attributed to the end of the "shadow baby boom"[7] generation's enrollment in undergraduate education and the resulting shrinkage in the pool of college-age students. Some of the decline is also attributable to the fact that a certain percentage of college-age students are choosing *alternatives* to traditional higher education; for example, some are seeking specialized technical training instead. This choice appears to be motivated, in part, by students' unwillingness to assume the high levels of educational debt associated with pursuing a 4-year undergraduate degree and by their skepticism that a college degree still remains as useful and valuable as it previously was in the job market.

The accelerating costs associated with higher education, including the cost of faculty and staff salaries and benefits as well as the cost of maintaining, building, and updating facilities, are the primary drivers of the increased overall cost of higher education, an increase that is well beyond the cost of living.[8] Many private, nonprofit higher education institutions are heavily tuition-driven, due to the fact that they are not well endowed and have limited ability to raise private support. As a result, they have little choice other than to raise tuition significantly—and frequently—and this has deterred many would-be applicants (and their parents) from seeking admission. This dilemma is not new, but it, too, was exacerbated by the COVID-19 pandemic.

Public higher education institutions, on the other hand, had certain obvious advantages during the turbulence of the pandemic period. Even though the flow of tax levy resources became somewhat more constrained as states struggled to cope with the large, unanticipated costs associated with the pandemic and with reduced tax revenues, there was never any serious doubt that state-supported colleges and universities would continue to receive annual budget allocations, even if they had to be reduced temporarily. As a result, recent tuition increases at most PHEIs have generally been modest, and many institutions have not raised tuition at all. It is important to note, however, that for most students attending PHIEs, *any* increase in tuition is highly consequential, given the limits on their family resources and their inability to take on large amounts of additional debt.

THE GROWING PUBLIC VS. PRIVATE COST GAP

Even setting aside the impact of the pandemic and the decline in the number of college-age students, one of the more distinctive trends in higher education over the past 2 decades has been a widening gap between the cost of attending a public versus a private, nonprofit institution. Table 8.1, which recapitulates the data presented in a different context in Table I.1 of the Introduction, provides a graphical representation of how these costs diverged just between 2000 and 2020. The table reveals that the cost of tuition and fees associated with attending a private college or university is increasing faster than the costs of tuition and fees at PHIEs, due to the factors cited earlier. Since these institutions obviously receive no public subsidy, they can only operate at a deficit for short periods and must therefore find a way to remain in or regain fiscal balance. In many cases, this leaves little choice other than to resort to annual tuition increases. The net result is that the total cost of attending many private, nonprofit institutions of higher education is moving beyond the economic reach of many middle-class families, even with scholarship aid and loans.

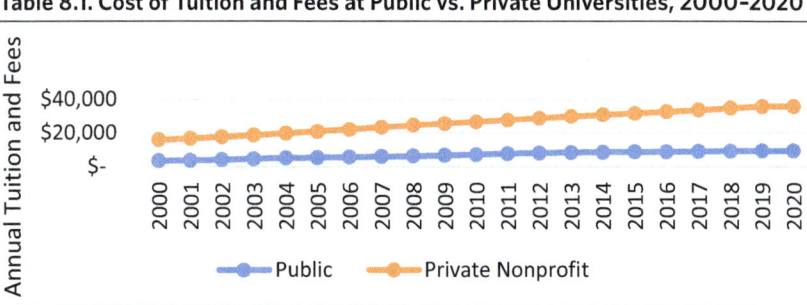

Table 8.1. Cost of Tuition and Fees at Public vs. Private Universities, 2000-2020

Source: U.S. Department of Education, National Center for Education Statistics, Integrated Postsecondary Education Data System (IPEDS) Fall Enrollment, 2000–2020

In many cases, parents are deciding that rather than saddling themselves and/or their students with a massive debt burden, which may require many years to repay, they will opt instead for a quality and affordable, publicly supported, higher education institutional alternatives. Thus, more and more families are deciding to have their student seek admission at a PHIE, and a highly ranked public college like Baruch, which has consistently received a top "Best Value" ranking, has witnessed a resulting surge in applications. Between 2014 and 2020 alone, Baruch's total applications increased by 24%—from 19,768 to 24,307 submissions.[9]

Private, nonprofit colleges and universities have pursued multiple strategies to try to remain competitive and to be able to continue to attract high-performing students, especially those from middle- and lower-income families, in the face of the demographic decline and escalation in costs. Their principal strategy has been to offer highly discounted tuition and to expand the availability of loans. In many cases, however, these loans are offered by private lenders at commercial rates, thereby adding to the student's and/or the family's debt burden, even in cases where they have also received a partial scholarship. It seems unlikely that the strategy of heavily discounting tuition can remain economically sustainable over the longer term, given that it reduces an institution's revenue and potentially increases its debt load.

The elite "Ivy-Plus" private schools across the country continue, of course, to receive plenty of applications from highly qualified applicants, including some from students who cannot possibly afford the total cost of attending the institution without substantial financial aid.[10] But private institutions lower down on the quality and prestige "food chain" have not fared as well in the competition for the reduced pool of college-age students, in part because they lack sufficient endowment and cannot afford to discount their tuition as deeply or offer as much financial aid.

If the economic gap between the cost of public versus private higher education continues to widen in the coming years, which seems likely, this will create the need for more institutions like Baruch—either that, or there will have to be entirely new *ways* of financing higher education. As I have noted, there are indications that middle-class families are no longer willing to assume the massive debt that is now required to pay for private college or university tuition and associated costs, even if they are discounted. If this trend continues, the number of students from lower-income families who attend private, nonprofit academic institutions will be substantially reduced, except where the student is lucky enough to be offered a full scholarship (i.e., tuition, room and board).

PROVIDING AN EDUCATED WORKFORCE FOR THE 21ST CENTURY

The U.S. public higher education system has served our country well since the land-grant universities were established in 1862 under the Morrill Act. It has helped to provide the educated workforce the United States required to keep it at the economic and technological leading edge. The PHIE system has propelled hundreds of thousands of people into the middle class, fundamentally changing the trajectory of their lives—and often the lives of their immediate families as well.

Many U.S. cities have also come to realize that PHIEs located within their municipal boundaries serve as primary engines of local economic development. They train the future workforce while also helping to reduce poverty and encourage upward socioeconomic mobility. They also provide administrative and academic jobs, which increases local employment and tax revenue. And they are a primary source of new ideas and startup companies that create *additional* jobs and further increase tax revenue for the city.

But the U.S. public higher education system is now under serious stress. Many PHIEs, Baruch among them, are either at or beyond their physical, financial, and academic limits;[11] they have neither the classroom space, the faculty resources, nor the operating budgets to admit additional undergraduates. It would be a serious error to allow these institutions, which have enabled students from diverse ethnic, racial, and economic backgrounds to gain the benefit of a higher education, to become overburdened and diminished in quality. PHEIs are the engine of our current and future economic and technical progress; allowing the system to deteriorate would be imperiling our progress as a nation.

REIMAGINING THE U.S. HIGHER EDUCATION SYSTEM

There appears to be little prospect or political appetite, at least in the near term, for fundamental change in the way that the U.S. higher education system (both public and private) is organized and financed. Thus, the only alternative may be to create (or expand) more PHIEs across the country, institutions that are organized, financed, and capable of performing in a manner similar to Baruch. Many such institutions *already exist* in the form of the large public universities that are to be found in every state in the nation. What is needed now is for more states to make a commitment to maintain affordable tuition (without the need for students to take on debt) and to improve educational outcomes, especially for students from low-income families. The state of California, for example, has created a *tiered* system of public colleges and universities and community colleges, each with their own distinct admission standards, cost structure, and mission. This three-tiered system is designed to accommodate as many students as possible across a wide range of socioeconomic status and academic achievement in the largest state in the union.[12]

Given the dramatic advances in science and technology (including especially computing, artificial intelligence, and advances in the life sciences), the changing global and domestic demand for skilled workers, the needs and aspirations of underrepresented minority communities, and the challenges already facing U.S. higher education that were previously enumerated in this volume, it can be argued that this is *exactly* the right moment to reconceive the entire higher education enterprise. But like so many other issues in today's highly polarized U.S. society, we have the spectacle of politicians attacking the U.S. higher education system, often very cynically, for its alleged "liberal bias," and passing laws to prevent certain subjects from even being taught on some campuses. Unfortunately, this leads inexorably to the conclusion that this is *not* the right time for a serious rethinking of how the U.S. higher education system is organized and financed. But I remain convinced that that day *will* come.

CONCLUSION

I have sought in this volume to identify the qualities and characteristics that have enabled one publicly supported college to advance academically, to remain financially stable, and to become an increasingly sought-after school for both undergraduate and graduate admissions. There seems to be little question that Baruch does represent at least an *informal* model for successful public higher education. As I have suggested, many of its elements and strategies can be replicated in other cities and states across the country by other publicly supported institutions that serve a diverse and largely low-income student population, and this can be accomplished in a manner that is appropriate to local political and economic conditions and constraints.

As I previously indicated, Baruch's emergence as a model for successful public education was in some respects accidental, since neither the leadership of the college nor the CUNY board of trustees ever set out to *make* it one. In fact, I doubt that such an idea was ever even seriously contemplated. From a financial standpoint, Baruch has achieved this success while being consistently shortchanged on its fair share of tuition resources, based on a per capita student allocation.[13] Yet, despite these impediments, the college has managed to remain financially stable, mainly by finding or developing new revenue streams that have enabled it to continue to deliver a quality education to its undergraduate and graduate students. And most importantly, despite having been significantly underfunded for years, Baruch students have continued to benefit from one of the lowest in-state tuition rates in the country and the state's Tuition Assistance Program.

I want to conclude by applauding the grit, determination, and generosity that has enabled Baruch's students and faculty, its administrators, and its private benefactors to achieve such great success over the years. In the end, there is nothing about the "Baruch model" that cannot be replicated successfully in other states and localities in some form or fashion, if the political will exists. Given that we now live in a domestic and international knowledge economy, it is increasingly urgent that we seek to fully engage and make use of our country's *entire* stock of human capital. To do so, we need successful public higher education institutions like Baruch College now more than ever.

Endnotes

Introduction

1. This is, of course, a reference to the famous children's book by the same name. Watty Piper, *The Little Engine That Could*, Penguin Random House LLC, 1930.

2. "Oldest public university in the United States," *Wikipedia*, February 22, 2022.

3. Ibid.

4. *The U.S. Land-Grant University System: Overview and Role in Agricultural Research*, Congressional Research Service, Updated August 9, 2022.

5. Ibid.

6. https://en.wikipedia.org/wiki/List_of_colleges_and_universities_in_the_United_States_by_endowment

7. It is also worth noting that "elite PIHEs" are not distributed evenly across the United States. Somewhat surprisingly, for example, the Northeast region has virtually none. This may perhaps be the result of the long tradition of elite private colleges and universities founded in the region, dating back to the 17th century. While there are many fine public universities in the Northeast, none of them enjoys the kind of large endowments possessed by the top state universities in other parts of the country. (Personal communication, Dr. David Birdsell, October 2023)

8. I am indebted to Dr. David Birdsell for helping to clarify this frame of reference.

9. See Dan Bauman, "Why Is West Virginia U. Making Sweeping Cuts? Hobbled by the Great Recession, the Flagship Bet on Growth That Never Came," *The Chronicle of Higher Education*, August 11, 2023.

10. Although not the focus of this volume, two good examples of such political pressure are (a) the campaigns that have been waged by the governors in Florida and several other states to prevent the teaching of Critical Race Theory in both secondary and tertiary institutions, and (b) the efforts by certain nongovernmental groups in some states to attack and try to end programs that support the LGBTQ communities and teach about related issues on public campuses.

11. The University of Texas system is perhaps the most notable exception, given that it has oil wealth.

12. This subject is addressed in detail in Chapter 1.

13. During the pandemic, CUNY (like most other higher education institutions, both public and private) suffered substantial enrollment declines. Interestingly,

Baruch College was the *only* academic element within CUNY that avoided this fate—in fact, its total enrollment actually increased slightly. Since the pandemic has moderated, enrollment at the CUNY senior colleges has begun increasing once again.

14. Unlike the federal government, states are not able to run budget deficits, since they do not possess the constitutional authority to print money or engage in deficit spending. They must therefore produce a balanced budget or find ways to eliminate the deficits.

15. CUNY is predominantly a commuter university, meaning that the vast majority of students live at home with their families or in group apartments. This makes the cost of pursuing a higher education degree at CUNY substantially less expensive than at many other public state universities, which may be located in a different part of the state and where students are expected to live on (or near) campus.

16. The ability of private institutions to achieve their desired racial and ethnic diversity goals was dealt a major blow, however, by the 2023 U.S. Supreme Court decision that blocked the use of affirmative action admissions based on race.

Chapter 1

1. Information for the description of the Free Academy was drawn largely from an online summary titled "CCNY—175 Years, Our History," https://www.ccny.cuny.edu/about/history; January 23, 2020.

2. Ibid.

3. Ibid.

4. Ibid.

5. The City College School of Business and Civic Administration was often referred to as "City Downtown," due to the fact that the main CCNY campus moved to Harlem, in upper Manhattan, in 1907.

6. I am indebted to Dr. David Birdsell for providing this insight. He also pointed out that the Fashion Institute of Technology (FIT), which is part of the State University of New York, is another public college in New York City that probably could not have been established anywhere else. Founded in 1944, FIT focuses exclusively on art, business, design, mass communication, and technology connected to the fashion industry and it serves the fashion industry, which is located in New York City.

7. The original community colleges that were part of CUNY were Staten Island Community College (now the College of Staten Island), 1956; Bronx Community College, 1957; Queensborough Community College, 1960; and Borough of Manhattan Community College and Kingsborough Community College in Brooklyn, 1963.

8. CUNY's Mission Statement is cited in the online description of the City University of New York; "About CUNY."

9. Source: https://studentaffairs.baruch.cuny.edu/starr-career-development-center/post-graduate-outcomes

10. Source: https://comptroller.nyc.gov/reports/cunys-contribution-to-the-economy

11. Information regarding the New York City fiscal crisis of 1975 is drawn from "History of New York City (1946–1977)," *Wikipedia*; www.en.wikipedia.org.

Endnotes

12. The term refers to schools that offered both a 2-year associate's degree and a 4-year bachelor's degree. In recent years, however, CUNY has been phasing out the 2-year degree at these colleges, and they are now all referred to as "senior colleges."

13. Noted in "The City University of New York," *Wikipedia*; www.en.wikipedia.org.

14. There are various theories about why this has been the case. Perhaps the most persuasive is that, by mutual agreement, all of the SUNY schools are located "upstate," where economic opportunities were increasingly limited as many companies moved their operations offshore. Governors who have appeared to favor SUNY may have been intent on limiting the economic impact in these cities and towns by maintaining and even expanding SUNY, which produced a substantial number of local jobs.

15. During the Cuomo years, when Bill de Blasio was the mayor of New York, the two leaders were frequently at odds and often barely on speaking terms. CUNY often bore the brunt of this political conflict, with the governor's office unwilling to agree to anything (like a budget increase) that would advance the interests of the mayor.

16. Stephen Steinberg, "Revisiting Open Admissions at CUNY," *The Clarion*, February 2018.

17. Ibid.

18. Ibid.

19. *The City University of New York: An Institution Adrift,* Report of the Mayor's Advisory Taskforce on The City University of New York, June 7, 1999.

20. I am indebted to Dr. Terrence Martell, the Saxe Distinguished Professor of Finance and Director Emeritus of the Weissman Center for International Business at Baruch College, for this insight.

21. CUNY FY 2020 Initial Operating Budget-Senior Colleges only.

22. Vivian Yee, "Cuomo to Continue Shrinking State's Share of CUNY's Costs," *The New York Times,* January 14, 2016.

23. Aaron Short, "Cuomo Wants to Join the State University of NY and CUNY," *The New York Post,* January 17, 2016.

24. The SUNY academic elements that are located in New York City are the SUNY Maritime College, the SUNY College of Optometry, the SUNY Empire College, the Fashion Institute of Technology, and the SUNY Global Center.

25. Since New York has historically been a "blue" state, Democratic governors have also tended to take the New York City voters for granted given the plurality of Democrats downstate.

26. The Professional Staff Congress, or PSC, is a faculty and staff union that represents both groups at CUNY in collective bargaining.

27. In fall 2013, CUNY implemented the Pathways initiative across all of the undergraduate colleges. Pathways established a new system of mandatory general education requirements and new transfer guidelines across the CUNY system.

28. Other liberal arts areas were seriously impacted, however. For example, foreign languages were hit hard.

29. I am indebted to Dr. Jessica Lang, the dean of the Weissman School of Arts and Sciences at Baruch, for her help and insight in reconstructing both the process and the outcome of this painful chapter.

Chapter 2

1. Baruch College Fact Sheet, fall 2020; also accessible at the following hyperlink: https://nam02.safelinks.protection.outlook.com/?url=https%3A%2F%2Fir.baruch.cuny.edu%2Fwp-content%2Fuploads%2Fsites%2F23%2F2021%2F01%2FFactsheet.Fall_2020_Finalx.pdf&data=05%7C02%7Cmitchel.wallerstein%40baruch.cuny.edu%7C56f811f7e64b40c67cc708dc5bc36e5e%7C6f60f0b35f064e099715989dba8cc7d8%7C0%7C0%7C638486142603820645%7CUnknown%7CTWFpbGZsb3d8eyJWIjoiMC4wLjAwMDAiLCJQIjoiV2luMzIiLCJBTiI6Ik1haWwiLCJXVCI6Mn0%3D%7C0%7C%7C%7C&sdata=Phg4PMwcH5j39UV9%2FKnNYf8jFyFzVRXxQj7EYu6BgSc%3D&reserved=0

2. A Pell Grant is money provided by the U.S. government to students based on financial need. The funds are grants, rather than loans, and they do not have to be repaid. Eligible students receive a specified amount each year while they remain academically and financially eligible. In the academic year of 2020–2021, about 30% of all undergraduates enrolled in the United States were awarded Pell Grants.

3. U.S. Department of Education, National Center for Education Statistics, Integrated Postsecondary Education Data System (IPEDS): Winter 2020–2021, Student Financial Aid component.

4. Baruch College Fact Sheet, fall 2020; Also available at the following hyperlink: https://nam02.safelinks.protection.outlook.com/?url=https%3A%2F%2Fir.baruch.cuny.edu%2Fwp-content%2Fuploads%2Fsites%2F23%2F2021%2F01%2FFactsheet.Fall_2020_Finalx.pdf&data=05%7C02%7Cmitchel.wallerstein%40baruch.cuny.edu%7C56f811f7e64b40c67cc708dc5bc36e5e%7C6f60f0b35f064e099715989dba8cc7d8%7C0%7C0%7C638486142603820645%7CUnknown%7CTWFpbGZsb3d8eyJWIjoiMC4wLjAwMDAiLCJQIjoiV2luMzIiLCJBTiI6Ik1haWwiLCJXVCI6Mn0%3D%7C0%7C%7C%7C&sdata=Phg4PMwcH5j39UV9%2FKnNYf8jFyFzVRXxQj7EYu6BgSc%3D&reserved=0

5. This was due, in large part, to the fact that the African American population in New York is concentrated in areas of the city where the high schools are underresourced and poorly performing, thereby making it difficult for many of these students to compete successfully for admission to Baruch.

6. Indeed, anti-Semitism remains a virulent problem worldwide in the 21st century, and it has been exacerbated by the rise of the extreme right, which includes white nationalist and other hate groups. It has even reemerged on some of the CUNY campuses (though not at Baruch), which is surprising and concerning given the presence of significant Jewish populations throughout most of the university.

7. I sometimes heard the statement from older alumni that "I went to Baruch because I had few other options, but my children didn't have to." They meant by this that thanks to the education they received and their own hard work and financial success, they became upwardly mobile and therefore able to send their children (and grandchildren) to many of the top private colleges and universities in the country.

8. Baruch College Fact Sheet, fall 2020; Also accessible at the following hyperlink: https://nam02.safelinks.protection.outlook.com/?url=https%3A%2F%2Fir

.baruch.cuny.edu%2Fwp-content%2Fuploads%2Fsites%2F23%2F2021 %2F01%2FFactsheet.Fall_2020_Finalx.pdf&data=05%7C02%7Cmitchel .wallerstein%40baruch.cuny.edu%7C56f811f7e64b40c67cc708dc5bc36e5e%7 C6f60f0b35f064e099715989dba8cc7d8%7C0%7C0%7C6384861426038206 45%7CUnknown%7CTWFpbGZsb3d8eyJWIjoiMC4wLjAwMDAiLCJQIjoiV2 luMzIiLCJBTiI6Ik1haWwiLCJXVCI6Mn0%3D%7C0%7C%7C%7C&sdata= Phg4PMwcH5j39UV9%2FKnNYf8jFyFzVRXxQj7EYu6BgSc%3D&reserved=0

9. This is not to suggest, of course, that there are not highly capable, academically qualified students enrolled in the other CUNY colleges. I am in this case only addressing the numbers for the overall pool of admitted students. It is also the case that the average combined SAT score and mean GPA for students admitted to CUNY's Macaulay Honors College in 2020 were 1414 and 94.1, respectively, which obviously far exceeds Baruch's numbers. But Macaulay, as a matter of policy, is focused on and exclusively admits only the highest-performing applicants.

10. Given the economic circumstances of most Baruch (and CUNY) students, and the fact that most must work either part- or full-time while attending college (and are often helping to support their family), it is often difficult for students to earn sufficient course credits to complete their degree requirements in less than 5–6 years.

11. Baruch College Fact Sheet, fall 2020; also available at the following hyperlink: https://nam02.safelinks.protection.outlook.com/?url=https%3A%2F% 2Fir.baruch.cuny.edu%2Fwp-content%2Fuploads%2Fsites%2F23%2F2021% 2F01%2FFactsheet.Fall_2020_Finalx.pdf&data=05%7C02%7Cmitchel .wallerstein%40baruch.cuny.edu%7C56f811f7e64b40c67cc708dc5b- c36e5e%7C6f60f0b35f064e099715989dba8cc7d8%7C0%7C0%7C638- 486142603820645%7CUnknown%7CTWFpbGZsb3d8eyJWIjoiMC4 wLjAwMDAiLCJQIjoiV2luMzIiLCJBTiI6Ik1haWwiLCJXVCI6Mn0% 3D%7C0%7C%7C%7C&sdata=Phg4PMwcH5j39UV9%2FKnNYf8jFyFzVRXx Qj7EYu6BgSc%3D&reserved=0

12. CollegeNET, Inc. (www.collegeNET.com) is a Portland, Oregon–based, privately held company providing web-based, on-demand technologies to colleges, universities, and nonprofits.

13. CollegeNET collects data from third-party sources, including the U.S. Department of Education's College Scorecard and IPEDS.

14. The average starting salary for students graduating from the Zicklin School of Business with a BBA is typically above $60,000.

15. Third Way (https://www.thirdway.org/about) is a national think tank that champions modern center-left ideas. Its work is grounded in the mainstream American values, but it identifies as center-left because it sees that space in U.S. politics as offering the only real path for advancing those ideals in the century ahead.

16. https://www.thirdway.org/report/out-with-the-old-in-with-the-new-rating -higher-ed-by-economic-mobility

17. Michael Itzkowitz, *Out With the Old, In With the New: Rating Higher Ed by Economic Mobility*, Third Way, January 27, 2022, https://www.thirdway .org/report/out-with-the-old-in-with-the-new-rating-higher-ed-by-economic-mobility. More information on how the Price-to-Earnings Premium is calculated can be found in "Providing Low-Income Students the Best Bang for Their Educational

Buck," located at https://www.thirdway.org/memo/providing-low-income-students-the-best-bang-for-their-educational-buck.

18. Admission to the BBA degree program in the Zicklin School of Business required, prior to 2021: (a) the successful completion of eight courses, which included (among other things) Calculus, English, Economics, and Statistics; and (b) the completion of at least 45 credits with a minimum GPA of at least 2.25 or higher.

19. Personal communication, Dr. H. Fenwick Huss, retired dean of the Zicklin School of Business, June 2023.

20. See Chapter 1.

21. Included in the estimate of undocumented students at Baruch, cited earlier in the chapter, are the DACA "Dreamers," who are currently ineligible to apply for citizenship.

22. Personal communication from Rosa Kelly, director of the International Student Services Center, Baruch College, July 2023.

23. Ibid.

24. This was the case up through AY19–20, after which the admission standard was modified to include a course in business statistics.

25. This is also the case, of course, for students admitted to Macaulay Honors College.

Chapter 3

1. The state of New York ranked #3 out of 50 in 2018 in direct support for higher education.

2. In fall 2013, CUNY implemented the Pathways initiative across its undergraduate colleges. Pathways established a new system of general education requirements and new transfer guidelines across CUNY.

3. During the COVID-19 pandemic, the number of transfer students seeking admission to Baruch dropped significantly. Also during this period, overall enrollment in community colleges nationwide dropped by double digits, which may partially explain the decline in transfers. As of this writing, it remains unclear whether the transfer numbers will return to their pre-pandemic levels, but the college considers the increased number of first-year students to be a net positive.

4. I am indebted to former Baruch Provost Dr. James McCarthy for this insight.

5. The Professional Staff Congress is the union that represents both faculty and staff at CUNY.

6. This point may not be universally true across all three of Baruch's schools, particularly if research and summer support is taken into account.

7. It is widely recognized that faculty compensation in medicine, law, science, engineering, and business is highly competitive and significantly higher than in other academic disciplines.

8. Admissions data provided by the Office of the Vice President for Enrollment Management, Baruch College.

9. Moderately selective colleges accept fewer than 60% of all applicants and possess an average composite ACT score of at least 25 or an average combined SAT score of at least 1210. (See www.CollegeTransitions.com.)

Endnotes

10. Data on SAT scores provided by the Office of the Vice President for Enrollment Management, Baruch College.

11. Data provided by the Office of the Director for Institutional Research, Hunter College.

12. SAT tests have now been made optional as an admission requirement at CUNY.

13. Source: https://nces.ed.gov/ipeds/datacenter/institutionprofile.aspx?unitId=190512&goToReportId=6

14. Many of Baruch's transfer students did not possess test scores and a grade profile when they graduated from high school that would make them eligible for admission directly to Baruch. It is a common story that most of these students therefore decided to enroll first at a community college, where they worked hard and were subsequently accepted to Baruch via transfer.

15. 2,256 students responded to the survey out of a total graduating class of 3,587. Data provided by the Office of the Director, Starr Career Development Center, Baruch College.

16. Ibid.

17. For example, *U.S. News and World Report*, The Princeton Review, and *Forbes*.

18. CUNY out-of-state undergraduate tuition is approximately double that of in-state tuition.

19. It has always struck me as regrettable that the southern end of the Baruch campus is located just one block north of the well-known Gramercy Park, which is one of the only *private*, gated parks in the city of New York. In fact, one must obtain (and pay for) a key to enter the park, which must be purchased by paying an annual fee. So the park remains inaccessible to the Baruch College community, just as it was in the days of the Free Academy in the 19th century.

Chapter 4

1. Total cost includes tuition, room, board, and related expenses (books, travel, etc.).

2. Education Data Initiative; www.educationdata.org; July 18, 2022.

3. Francesca Maglione, "Ivy League Prices Are Pushing $90,000 a Year," *Bloomberg*, www.bloomberg.com, March 28, 2023.

4. Ron Lieber, "Some Colleges Will Soon Charge $100,000 a Year. How Did This Happen?," *The New York Times*, April 8, 2024.

5. As I previously have noted, there are exceptions to this point among PHEIs. The University of Texas system, for example, has the great advantage of owning substantial oil resources and has an estimated endowment of approximately $42 billion.

6. Under the sharing arrangement agreed upon when financial responsibility for the CUNY senior colleges was transferred from the city to the state, in the aftermath of the New York City financial crisis in the 1970s, the governor appoints two-thirds of the CUNY Board of Trustees, and the mayor appoints one-third. While this does give the governor a majority controlling interest, it differs from the governance of SUNY, where the governor appoints the entire board.

7. The University of California system, which is at the top of the academic pyramid in the state of California, includes campuses such as Berkeley, Los

Angeles, San Diego, San Francisco, Davis, and a number of others. All of the schools are R1 research institutions.

8. The California state system represents the second tier of the California higher education system. It includes campuses at San Jose, San Luis Obispo, Fresno, Chico, and others.

9. I am indebted to Dr. David Birdsell, the provost at Kean State University in New Jersey, for identifying these points.

10. And it so happens that the SUNY Chancellery is located within *eyesight* of the state legislature and governor's office, while the CUNY Chancellery is more than 150 miles away in New York City.

11. In the state of New York, the final budget deal is the product of what is often referred to as "Three Men in a Room," meaning that it results from a series of closed-door meetings between the governor, the Senate Majority Leader, and the Speaker of the Assembly. In recent years, however, two of the these three leadership positions were held by women.

12. Since the pandemic, even this assumption is changing, since many courses are now offered fully online.

13. A former Baruch athletic director once commented to me about the difficulty of getting students to turn out to support college teams at big sports events: "A student who lives out in the far end of Queens and has to pay to ride the subway for more than hour each way to get to/from Baruch is just not going to make a second trip back to the campus after attending class and then going to his/her job and returning home. They understand that it's just not a productive use of their time, and it's also expensive when they are living on a very limited budget."

14. I am indebted to Baruch VP for Student Affairs Art King for sharing these points with me.

15. Tragically, there were a number of undergraduate suicides that occurred during my 10-year tenure as president. Almost all of them took place off campus. In most of the cases, the students were known to the college's Counseling Center, but a few were not.

16. Occasionally, it is the parent who alerts the college to a student who is struggling. But this is unusual.

17. The PSC was established in 1972, and soon thereafter it won the right to bargain collectively on behalf of 30,000 faculty and certain categories of staff across CUNY's 25 campuses.

18. The other new labor challenge on many campuses is the situation of doctoral students, who often are called on to teach or to provide labor in support a faculty mentor's research. They, too, have been making efforts to unionize. It remains unclear whether these groups will become integrated into the existing faculty union, or if they will remain separate given that they represent a narrow and somewhat atypical slice of the academic workforce.

19. It has often been the case in recent years, however, that contract negotiations have become bogged down and protracted, sometimes requiring a process lasting years. In fact, one recent contract negotiation required fully *6 years* to settle. As a result, employees have had to accept being paid based on the terms of a long-expired contract while negotiations continued.

Endnotes

20. For example, the PSC has adopted resolutions on the verdict of the George Floyd murder trial, on anti-Asian violence, and expressing opposition to a "new Cold War" with China.

21. CUNY Professional Staff Congress, Delegate Assembly, "Resolution in Support of the Palestinian People," adopted on June 10, 2021.

22. Scott Jaschik, "Division in CUNY Faculty Union," *Inside Higher Education*, July 22, 2021.

23. Given the location of the "17 Lex" building, over the years students often jocularly referred to it as "UCLA—the university at the corner of Lexington Avenue."

24. Two of the buildings on the "south campus" were previously New York City courthouses, which were later given to CUNY and repurposed to serve the needs of Baruch College.

25. Karen W. Arenson, "Baruch College Opens a Huge 'Vertical Campus,'" *The New York Times*, August 28, 2001.

26. The actual net usable space is 800,000 square feet.

27. Ibid.

28. Personal communication, CUNY Office of Facilities Planning, Construction, and Management, 2012.

29. Baruch's main academic building is called the "Newman Vertical Campus," which is an indication of the verticality of the school's facilities and of the fact that there is simply no room to build horizontally in a densely populated and fully developed, urban environment, unlike the situation at most colleges and universities with discrete, self-contained campuses.

30. The Newman Vertical Campus building was actually designed and built with several outdoor terraces, all ultimately had to be closed due to security concerns.

31. One of the most well-known parks in the area, Gramercy Park, was established more than a hundred years ago as a *private* park that required the payment of an annual membership fee in order to obtain a key to unlock the gates. As such, this park remains unavailable to this day to local residents who are not members, which of course includes the Baruch College community.

32. The commitment of public funds became essential when it was discovered that the water and sewer pipes running underneath the block of 25th Street in question were more than 100 years old and had to be replaced before a plaza could be developed. This cost was well beyond the financial capacity of Baruch College, and it was, in any case, the responsibility of the city. Ultimately, New York City paid for the *underground* portion of the work and the college raised the private funds needed to pay for the *surface* landscaping work.

33. The college employed a variety of initiatives to raise the private match. First, it was fortunate to have a group of generous alumni donors who set the example by making major gift commitments. The leaders of this initiative were the (late) Lawrence Field and Daniel Clivner, both of whom actually resided in Los Angeles. Together, the group of major donors contributed more than $2.5 million toward the surface cost of the plaza. The second part of the strategy involved enabling individual alumni and friends of the college to contribute through the purchase of engraved "paver" stones. At the end of the campaign, which was led

most ably by the college's Vice President for College Advancement, David Shanton, 1,462 pavers had been purchased, which provided an additional $677,527. The grand total of private funds raised in support of Clivner=Field Plaza was $3,376,708. To the best of our knowledge, the Baruch plaza was the first in the city to be developed as a public-private partnership.

34. I want here to acknowledge and thank three senior members of the Baruch College President's Cabinet, who each played a critical role in helping bring this project to fruition through their dedicated work, which extended over many years: Vice President for Administration and Facilities Katharine Cobb (now retired); Vice President for College Advancement David Shanton; and then Vice President for Communications, Marketing, and Public Affairs Christina Latouf.

35. Baruch Annual Report 2019–2020; https://www.alumni.baruch.cuny.edu/uploaded/Annual_Reports/BCFAnnualReportFY20-FinalV2.pdf?1645324128596

36. Council for Advancement and Support of Education, *CASE Insights on Alumni Engagement: Key Findings,* 2022.

37. These donors were Lawrence Zicklin—the Zicklin School of Business, George and Mildred Weissman—the Weissman School of Arts and Sciences, and Austin Marxe—the Marxe School of Public and International Affairs.

Chapter 5

1. This view can be traced back to the decision taken during New York City's financial crisis in the 1970s when the state of New York was forced to assume financial responsibility for most of CUNY's 4-year institutions. See Chapter 1.

2. Personal communication, Office of the Vice President for Enrollment Management, Baruch College, August 2023.

3. www.BestColleges.com, 2023.

4. Given that most Baruch students work, either part- or full-time, during their undergraduate years, it is quite common for them to require more than 4 years to complete their degrees. Many are paying their own way through college, or they may be a breadwinner for their extended family, and/or they may have families of their own. Under any of these scenarios, a longer time to graduation may be necessary.

5. I am indebted to Dr. H. Fenwick Huss, the distinguished former dean of the Zicklin School of Business, who generously provided the detailed information presented in this section.

6. The original Zicklin MBA program required 57 credits to complete and had 10 different specializations. After a comprehensive faculty study of the top MBA program curricula, the number of required credits was reduced to 45–48 and the number of options simplified. In the end, a student-centric, career-focused MBA curriculum emerged with 48 credits, divided into foundational knowledge, functional knowledge, and career-focused electives.

7. With this innovative program structure, the Zicklin School of Business launched the new dual degree programs, starting in 2017, with the following institutions: (1) MBA-MS in Finance with HSBC School of Business of Peking University, China; (2) MBA-MS in Finance with the School of Business of Renmin University, China; (3) MBA-MS in Finance with the School of Business of Beijing University of Science & Technology, China; (4) MBA-MS in Finance

Endnotes

with the School of Business of Xi'an Jiaotong University, China; (5) MBA-MS in Finance with the School of Business of Shanghai University of International Studies, China; (6) MBA-MS in Finance with the Free University of Bozen-Bolzano, Italy; (7) MBA-MS in Finance with the University of Padova, Italy; and (8) MBA-MS in Entrepreneurship with College of Management Studies of Tel Aviv, Israel.

8. The average starting salary for the 2023 graduates of the MFE graduate program was almost $168,000.

9. QuantNet, *2021 Ranking of Best Financial Engineering Programs*, https://quantnet.com/2021-mfe-programs-rankings/

10. As this volume was being completed, Risk.net announced its new Quant Finance Worldwide Ranking, in which Baruch College toppled Princeton University for the first time to attain the #1 *international* ranking. According to the Risk.net announcement, "Since Risk.net began producing its guide to the world's leading quantitative finance master's programmes in 2016, Princeton had reigned supreme. This year, the Ivy League school was displaced by a public college: The City University of New York's Baruch College." (Personal communication from Professor Dan Stefanica, director of the Baruch Master of Financial Engineering program, May 20, 2023.)

11. The four major academic concentration areas in the MIA program are: (a) international nongovernmental organizations, (b) trade policy and global economic governance, (c) Western Hemispheric affairs, and (d) global security.

12. Like virtually all academic programs in CUNY and elsewhere, application numbers declined during the pandemic, but have since begun to recover.

13. Baruch College is the only college in the CUNY system to have all of its major academic units named and endowed.

14. The two exceptions are City and Hunter Colleges, both of which are much older than Baruch, dating back to the 19th century. Both have therefore benefited from many years of endowment and testamentary gifts from their alumni/ae. City College also is the location of CUNY's primary engineering and medical programs, which also have produced alumni with the financial capacity to give back. For example, in 2005, Andrew Grove, one of the founders of the Intel corporation, made a $25 million gift to City College to underwrite its engineering programs.

15. Both CUNY and SUNY maintain a policy whereby administrative staff receive the equivalent of tenure after seven years of satisfactory service, meaning that they only can be dismissed for cause. As a result, neither tenured faculty nor staff can be laid off unless the university declares "fiscal exigency," which it has done only once in its history.

16. I am indebted to Katharine Cobb, the now-retired vice president of Baruch College for Administration and Finance, for her expert and detailed summary of the administrative strategies employed by the college during this period, which are described in this section. Personal communication, July 2023.

17. Vacancy savings are cost reductions derived from vacant faculty and staff positions, usually as a result of a retirement or resignation or a research leave (if undertaken with external funding).

18. Mandatory needs are legal obligations, such as the cost of salary step increases, that are built into labor contracts.

19. This problem is especially severe due given that Baruch College consists of seven vertical buildings, some as tall as 17 stories. Thus, when old and overused elevators break down, there are immediately long lines of students and faculty waiting to ascend, which is highly problematic during class change periods. It is also makes things particularly difficult for those with physical disabilities to get to classes on time.

20. The consummation of the deal was aided considerably by the assistance of and pressure brought to bear by the Office of Senator Charles Schumer (D-NY).

21. Summary of rankings drawn from the Baruch College website: https://nam02.safelinks.protection.outlook.com/?url=https%3A%2F%2Fnewscenter.baruch.cuny.edu%2Fnews%2Fbaruch-college-earns-top-rankings-2022%2F&data=05%7C02%7Cmitchel.wallerstein%40baruch.cuny.edu%7Cfc662757d6ce44e9f2b408dc5d8068f2%7C6f60f0b35f064e099715989dba8cc7d8%7C0%7C0%7C638488053314855068%7CUnknown%7CTWFpbGZsb3d8eyJWIjoiMC4wLjAwMDAiLCJQIjoiV2luMzIiLCJBTiI6Ik1haWwiLCJXVCI6Mn0%3D%7C0%7C%7C%7C&sdata=xcozoSWewRtspfVhD7xYTpDeEIxfvN2ML0VLedlMQf0%3D&reserved=0

22. See Frank Bruni, "There's Only One College Rankings List That Matters," *The New York Times,* March 27, 2023.

Chapter 6

1. Founded in 1847, the City College of New York is the oldest school in the CUNY system, and it was all-male until the middle of the 20th century. Hunter College is the second-oldest school, founded in 1870 as a women's college.

2. This advantage is shared with Hunter College, which is about 40 blocks to the north along Lexington Avenue.

3. Personal communication, Office of the Vice President for College Advancement, Baruch College, August 2023.

4. I am indebted to Dr. David Birdsell for sharing this insight.

5. I am indebted to Dr. Myung-Soo Lee for sharing this insight.

6. According to the PSC website, "The Professional Staff Congress . . . represents 30,000 faculty and staff at the City University of New York (CUNY) and the CUNY Research Foundation. The union negotiates, administers, and enforces collective bargaining agreements; protects the rights of staff through the grievance and arbitration process; engages in political activity on behalf of CUNY and its staff and students; and advocates for the interests of the instructional staff in its various forums. It also provides benefits and services to its members through such related organizations as the PSC/CUNY Welfare fund and New York State United Teachers (NYSUT)."

7. Personal communication, Office of the Vice President for College Advancement, Baruch College, August 2023.

8. Kaplan, E. Anne, Council for Advancement and Support of Education. (2022). "Voluntary Support of Education 2020–2021," *AMAtlas,* www.case.org; Kaplan, E. Anne, Council for Advancement and Support of Education (2022). "CASE Alumni Engagement Metrics Key Findings, 2021," *AMAtlas,* www.case.org

9. The Executives on Campus (EOC) program at Baruch is a mentoring activity that connects undergraduate and graduate students with senior individu-

Endnotes

als with extensive experience in business and nonprofit organizations. Mentors provide guidance to students in networking, interviewing, and other essential business etiquette skills to make them competitive in today's job market.

10. In the early years of the business school, private companies saw Baruch students as fit only for jobs in accounting, HR, and other so-called "back of the house" positions. But in the past decade, these attitudes have changed significantly. Today, Baruch business graduates compete for "C-suite–track" jobs in finance and management. In part, this change was due to the increased academic rigor of the Zicklin School's curriculum and also due to a growing recognition that Baruch graduates are well trained and ready to work on day 1. The fact that most had already been working during college and graduate school is now also seen as a plus.

11. Office of the New York City Comptroller, 2021, "CUNY's Contribution to the Economy: CUNY Graduates in the Workforce," https://comptroller.nyc.gov/reports/cunys-contribution-to-the-economy/#cuny-graduates-in-the-workforce, March 12, 2021.

Chapter 7

1. Now defunct, the New York City Board of Higher Education previously oversaw the city's public institutions, including the senior colleges and community colleges that later became part of CUNY. The board was disestablished in 1979.

2. This history was described in Chapter 1.

3. Elements of what became the State University of New York (SUNY) were established at roughly the same time as the Free Academy, which was the precursor to the City University of New York (CUNY). The University of Buffalo, for example, was created in 1846 and the University of Albany in 1844.

4. I am indebted to Dr. David Birdsell for providing this insight about SUNY and CUNY.

5. I am indebted to Professor Carol Berkin, Baruch Presidential Professor of History Emeritus, for sharing this insight.

6. Beginning in 2022, students in the BBA degree program may now also complete a second *major* concentration in the liberal arts, based on the requirements for a major in a department of the Weissman School of Arts and Sciences.

7. CUNY tried for a number of years during my tenure to pursue a policy of "predictable tuition increases," which were very modest annual increases that were designed to avoid a much larger tuition adjustment in future years. But even this approach was ultimately opposed as slowly pricing the university out of reach for the most economically limited students. This caused the CUNY board to announce a cessation in tuition increases, even though this policy is not financially sustainable.

8. In addition to the Zicklin School of Business at Baruch College, which is nationally ranked, there is also the Murray Koppelman School of Business at Brooklyn College and the Lucille and Jay Chazanoff School of Business at the College of Staten Island.

9. As I have noted, it is also the case that faculty for graduate degree programs, both the MBA and the PhD, are extremely expensive, and it would make little sense for other CUNY colleges to try to duplicate this capability elsewhere in the same university.

10. This strategy is now being used extensively in many states. The state of Vermont, which is ranked last in the table, has perhaps the widest differential between in-state and out-of-state tuition rates. In New York State, undergraduate tuition for out-of-state students is double the in-state rate.

Chapter 8

1. See, for example, Susan Wright and Chris Shore, eds., *Death of the Public University: Uncertain Futures for Higher Education in the Knowledge Economy,* Berghahn Books, 2017; Elizabeth M. Holcombe, Adrianna J. Kezar, Susan L. Elrod, and Judith A. Ramaley, *Shared Leadership in Higher Education: A Framework and Models for Responding to a Changing World,* Taylor & Francis, 2023; John R. Thelin, *American Higher Education: Issues and Institutions,* Taylor & Francis, 2022; Jason Wingard, *The College Devaluation Crisis: Market Disruption, Diminishing ROI, and an Alternative Future of Learning,* Stanford Business Books, Stanford University Press, 2022.

2. Lederman, Doug, August 1, 2021, "Number of Colleges Shrinks Again, Including Public and Private Nonprofits," *Inside Higher Ed,* https://www.insidehighered.com/news/2021/08/02/number-colleges-shrinks-again-including-publics-and-private-nonprofits

3. Leif Weatherby, "What Just Happened at West Virginia University Should Worry All of Us," *The New York Times,* August 20, 2023.

4. Anemona Hartocollis, "Slashing Its Budget, West Virginia University Asks, What Is Essential?," *The New York Times,* August 18, 2023.

5. Ibid.

6. Legacy admission is the offer of enrollment to the children, grandchildren, or other relatives of alumni, particularly those who have been generous donors to a university or college.

7. The "shadow baby boom" refers to the *children* of the post–World War II baby boom generation, who caused a bulge in higher education enrollment similar to that which occurred in the 1960s and early 1970s when their "baby boom" parents came of age to attend college.

8. Perhaps not surprisingly, the problem of rapidly rising education costs was exacerbated by the high inflation that began during the COVID-19 pandemic.

9. Source: National Center for Education Statistics.

10. A recent study by Raj Chetty, David J. Deming, and John N. Friedman found that elite colleges and universities (meaning the Ivy League, plus schools such as Stanford, Duke, and the University of Chicago) are more than twice as likely to admit a student from a high-income family over a student from a low- or middle-income family with comparable SAT/ACT scores. According to the authors, attending one of these institutions *triples* a student's chances of obtaining a job at a prestigious firm and substantially increases their chances of earning in the top 1%. Raj Chetty, David J. Deming, and John N. Friedman, "Diversifying Society's Leaders? The Determinants and Consequences of Admission to Highly Selective Colleges," *Opportunity Insights,* July 2023.

11. I use the term *academic limits* here to suggest the constraints imposed on PHEIs by state governments in terms of the number of faculty that a particular college or university is authorized to hire and employ.

12. The state of California supports the University of California system, the California State University system, and the California Community College system, totaling more than 150 colleges and universities in all.

13. CUNY employs an allocation formula for the distribution of tuition that is *not* based on the number of students enrolled in a particular college. This means that, in reality, many of the financially challenged campuses in CUNY are cross-subsidized by the more successful schools because they receive more than their fair share on a per capita basis of the total tuition paid by CUNY's 240,000+ students each year. In fact, the data reveal that Baruch receives the *smallest* allocation of tuition dollars in CUNY on a per capita basis.

Index

Academic excellence fees, 66
Adjunct faculty, 13, 47
Affirmative action, 94, 102n16
African American students, 22, 88–90, 104n5
Anti-Semitism, 55, 77, 104n6
Asian-American students, 21–22, 88–90
Author's experiences, 57–58

Badillo, Herman, 15
Baruch, Bernard M., 11, 64
Baruch College
   academic focus/quality, 28–29, 31–32, 33–37, 76
   academic innovation, 61–64
   academic supports, 60–61, 80–81
   admissions policies, 15, 35
   Annual Fund, 56
   "Baruch model," 7, 85–91
   as commuter school, 24, 46–47
   compared to similar colleges/universities, 38–42
   endowments, 64–65
   financial stability, 65–69
   history and overview, 11–20
   Manhattan location, 50–51, 73
   mission, 74–75
   Newman Vertical Campus, 49–50, 109nn29–30
   physical facilities and space constraints, 49–53, 69–70, 112n19
   and political issues, 76–77
   private companies/nonprofit organizations, campus presence, 80
   private fundraising, 78–79
   rankings, national and regional, 70–71
   relationship to CUNY, 18–19, 90–91
   success of, 83–85
   tuition and affordability, 37–38
   visibility of, 71–72
   "vocational" vs. liberal arts curricula, 85
   See also Marxe School of Public and International Affairs; Weissman School of Arts and Sciences; Zicklin School of Business
Baruch College Conference Center, 68
Baruch College faculty and staff, 75–76
   recruitment, 34–35
   salaries, 29, 35
   union activism, 48–49, 77–78
Baruch College Fund (BCF), 51, 55, 64–65, 78–79
Baruch College student body, 75
   demographics and diversity, 21–24, 25, 88–90
   enrollment, 51, 66, 106n3
   international students, 29–30
   Jewish students, 55–56
   post-graduation activity, 30–31, 37
   qualifications, 59–60
   socioeconomic status, 24–28
   student academic quality, 35–37
   Student Government Association, 52
   transfer students, 33–34, 106n3, 107n14
   working students, 46–47

Baruch College Writing Center, 60
Baruch Plaza, 53
Bernard Baruch Dinner, 56
Bernard L. Schwartz Communication Institute, 60
Birdsell, David, 102n6
Bloomberg, Michael, 52
Boycott, Divestment, and Sanctions (BDS) movement, 49
Brooklyn College, 11
Business students/curricula. *See* Zicklin School of Business

California
   California State University, 39–42
   tax funds for public universities, 88
   tiered higher education system, 98, 107–108nn7–8
Chetty, Raj, 27
City University of New York (CUNY)
   academic innovation, 61
   Board of Trustees, 15
   budget crisis (2010–2011), 65–66
   challenges and criticisms, 57–58
   as commuter university, 102n15
   comparison of similar colleges/universities, 39–42
   contrasted with Baruch, 84
   demographics and diversity, 21–24
   free tuition, withdrawal of, 12–13
   funding issues, 15–18
   history and overview, 9–20, 102n7
   Jewish students, 55
   minority admissions, 14–15
   New York City fiscal crisis (1975), 12–13, 15–16
   open admissions policies, 14–15, 23
   political support for, 43–45
   structure and organization, 18–20, 57–58, 73, 90–91
   tuition and affordability, 4–5, 37–38, 113n7
   undocumented students, 22
   unionized faculty/staff, 47–48, 77–78
   working class, outreach to, 9–10
   See also Baruch College

The City University of New York: An Institution Adrift, 15
Clivner=Field Plaza, 53, 109–110n33
College of William & Mary, 1
COVID-19 pandemic, 46, 51–52, 94–95, 101–102n13, 106n3
Cuomo, Andrew, 13, 16–17, 44, 77, 103n15
Curricular uniformity, 19–20

De Blasio, Bill, 103n15
Doctoral programs, 61–62
Dual-degree programs, 62–63, 110–111n7

Economic Mobility Index (EMI), 26–28, 37–38
Elite institutions, 43, 101n7, 114n10
Endowments, 55, 64–65
Energy savings, 69

Faculty
   adjunct, 13, 47
   hiring process, 68
   salary supplements, 68
Fashion Institute of Technology (FIT), 102n6
Financial Engineering programs, 63
Florida State University, 39–42
Free Academy, 4, 9–10, 84

G.I. Bill, 11
Giuliani, Rudolph, 15
Goldstein, Matthew, 15, 49, 59
Graduate programs, 61–64
Gramercy Park, 38, 49, 50, 107n19, 109n31
Great Recession (21st century), 3, 13, 65
Great Works of Literature program, 19, 34

Harris, Townsend, 9, 10
Hispanic students, 22, 88–90
Hostos Community College, 20
Hunter College, 11

# Index

Illinois, 45
Israel, support for, 49
Ivy League schools, 43, 114n10

Jewish students, 23, 55, 88

Land grant universities, 1–2, 84
Latino students, 22, 88–90
Lindsay, John, 14

Macaulay Honors College, 23, 35, 58, 73, 105n9
Marxe, Austin W., 65
Marxe School of Public and International Affairs, 28, 29
  academic innovation, 63–64
Master's programs, 62, 63–64
Matos Rodriguez, Félix, 20
Morrill Act (1862), 1, 97
Municipal Assistance Corporation (MAC), 12

Newman, William, 56
Newman Vertical Campus, 49–50, 109nn29–30
New York City
  Board of Higher Education, 14
  fiscal crisis (1975), 12–13
  Gramercy park, 38, 49, 50, 107n19, 109n31
  immigrant populations and minorities, 14, 38, 84
  Plaza Program, 52
New York State
  "upstate vs. downstate" problem, 17–18
  See also State University of New York (SUNY)

Palestinian people, support for, 49
Pathways initiative, 19, 33–34
Pell Grants, 21, 27–28, 37, 40, 104n2
Penn State University, 93
Position management, 67
Poverty
  CUNY students, 4, 11, 21
  public higher education institutions (PHEIs), 97

Price-to-Earnings Premium (PEP), 27–28, 40, 83
Private fundraising/philanthropy, 53–56, 88–89
Professional Staff Congress (PSC), 35, 47–49, 77–78
Protest, campus, 14
Public higher education institutions (PHEIs)
  affordability and accessibility, 11–12
  contemporary challenges, 2–3, 83
  enrollment patterns, 6–7, 94
  future of, reflections on, 93–99
  overview and history, 1–2
  political pressures on, 101n10
  political support for, 43–45
  and private philanthropy, 53–56
  public vs. private cost gap, 95–96
  state-by-state funding levels, 3–4
  tuition levels, 4–6
  viability of "Baruch model," 87–88

Queens College, 11, 20

Race-based affirmative action, 94, 102n16
Rockefeller, Nelson A., 11
Rohatyn, Felix G., 12
Rutgers University, 93–94

SAT scores, 59–60
Schmidt, Benno, Jr., 15
Social Mobility Index (SMI), 25–26, 37–38, 71, 85
Southwest University for Finance and Economics (SWUFE), 30
Starr Career Development Center, 60
State University of New York (SUNY)
  comparison of similar colleges/universities, 39–42
  "flagship" campuses, 20
  history of, 84
  structure, 103n14
Steinberg, Stephen, 14
Student Academic Consulting Center, 60

Texas, public higher education institutions (PHEIs), 3–4, 88
Third Way (NGO), 26–27, 105n15
Tools for Clear Speech program, 60
Tuition, 85–86
 at elite institutions, 43
 New York City fiscal crisis (1975), 12–13
 public vs. private, 4–6
Tuition Assistance Program (TAP), 4, 12–13, 21, 26, 86
Tzedakah tradition, 55

University of California (UC) system, 20
 funding for, 44
University of Georgia, 1
University of Illinois, Chicago, 39–42
University of Maryland, Baltimore, 39–42
University of Michigan, 2
University of North Carolina, 1
University of Texas, 2, 39–42
University of Virginia, 2

Vacancy savings policies, 66–67

Webster, Dr. Horace, 9, 10
Weissman School of Arts and Sciences, 28, 29
 academic innovation, 63
 faculty salaries, 48
West Virginia University, 93

Zicklin School of Business
 academic innovation, 61–63
 admission requirements, 31–32
 curricular requirements, 34
 dual degree programs, 62–63, 110–111n7
 enrollment statistics, 28–29
 exchange programs, 30
 faculty salaries, 29, 48
 Great Works program, 19
 students' families, impact on, 73–74
 student socioeconomic status, 26

About the Author

Mitchel Wallerstein has had a long and distinguished career in academia, philanthropy, government, and the nonprofit policy sector. He served as the president of Baruch College of The City University of New York (CUNY) for 10 years (2010–2020), and he is now president emeritus and appointed as a University Professor at CUNY and Baruch. Prior to joining Baruch, Dr. Wallerstein was the dean of the Maxwell School of Citizenship and Public Affairs at Syracuse University (2003–2010). He previously served as vice president of the John D. and Catherine T. MacArthur Foundation (1998–2003), and before that as Deputy Assistant Secretary of Defense (1993–1998). Wallerstein received his PhD and MS degrees from MIT, an MPA degree from the Maxwell School at Syracuse, and an AB degree from Dartmouth College. He is an elected Fellow of the National Academy of Public Administration and of the American Association for the Advancement of Science, and he is a lifetime member of the Council on Foreign Relations.